MW00892383

Disclaimer: The opinions presented herein are solely those of the author except where specifically noted. Nothing in the book should be construed as investment advice or guidance, as it is not intended as investment advice or guidance, nor is it offered as such. Nothing in the book should be construed as a recommendation to buy or sell any financial or physical asset. It is solely the opinion of the writer, who is not an investment professional. The strategies presented in the book may be unsuitable for you, and you should consult a professional where such consultation is appropriate. The publisher/author disclaims any implied warranty or applicability of the contents for any particular purpose. The publisher/author shall not be liable for any commercial or incidental damages of any kind or nature.

First edition published September 2013

Oftwominds.com
P.O. Box 4727
Berkeley, California 94704

Copy editing: Jill Kanter
Cover design: Elena Gallmeier

The Nearly Free University and the Emerging Economy:
The Revolution in Higher Education

Charles Hugh Smith

With gratitude to Peter Kleinhans and the oftwominds.com subscribers and contributors who collectively enabled the writing of this book.

Table of Contents

Foreword by Mark A. Gallmeier

Change is a most difficult challenge for many people. It is even more difficult for people in groups. The Nearly Free University model represents such a change, an entirely new method of education.

Developments in education and information media have always impacted each other. Below is a brief review of the history of each for the past 2,500 years. The aim is to open minds as to how the asymptotic expansion of the information media technology known as the Internet is expanding education beyond its previous boundaries.

Brief History of Educational Media

Archimedes independently derived the Fundamental Theorem of Calculus over 2,300 years ago. This theorem did not become widely known until recently because of the scarcity of media, specifically papyrus and vellum parchments. During the time of the Roman Empire, the Library of Alexandria and the Roman imperial bureaucracy consumed almost the entire annual production of papyrus in Egypt. In fact, the competing library at Pergamum in Anatolia developed the use of vellum parchment specifically because of a lack of papyrus.

The extreme shortage of written media caused learning to become focused on two customs. One was the primacy of the oral lecture, such as Hero's lectures on mechanisms. The other was the requirement to concentrate students in one small geographic area to hear these lectures.

Due to the concentration of all this academic information in one place with limited access, the libraries tended to become centers of academic study and scientific research. Thus ancient colleges and universities first developed in parallel with the ancient libraries, for obvious reasons.

Development of the Oral Lecture

Many surviving ancient books began as sets of written lecture notes. Many other books, such as the New Testament, began as letters addressed from one person or group to another. An especially well-endowed library might have as many as 500 books, each produces by scribes, by hand, a single copy at a time. Due to the lack of time and papyrus/vellum, it was impossible to provide every student with their own set of textbooks. Instead, students were assembled in a room to hear a professor read to them from the school's single book copy. It is notable that one of the most ancient of present-day universities, Cambridge University in England, to this day preserves the memory of this practice with the formal academic rank of "Reader."

The ancient oral lecture method of delivering information is still in use at most universities, but is now subject to what I call the Johnny Carson Principle, which states "there is and can be only one Johnny Carson." Within a talented, diverse field of talk-show hosts, only one host occupies the top spot. Applying this principle to the education filed, in any given field there will only be a handful of truly A-list lecturers, but with one clearly at the head of the pack.

In my view, Dr. Walter Lewin of MIT is clearly the Johnny Carson of Physics I & II. His Physics lectures—which are theatrical-grade productions—are readily available on YouTube. Note that unrivalled genius in theoretical research is no guarantee of being an excellent physics lecturer and educator.

Where We Are Today

Two thousand years later the modern college and university is clearly still structured around the ancient principles. Even the appearance and spread of Gutenberg's printing press in the 15th century simply served to multiply the numbers of schools organized on this ancient pattern. Currently two primary elements of the old style system, written media and oral lectures, are already widely available at greatly reduced cost. The Nearly Free University (NFU) already exists in a practical sense. One example of open-access curriculum will suffice: the study of physics for science and engineering majors. Free, professional-level materials for Newtonian mechanics and subsequent developments in electrical, optical and nuclear physics are available online at numerous websites. Yet science and engineering continue to be taught using the ancient system, using well-paid professors and expensive university classrooms to teach physically present students.

Despite major advances in media technology and the accompanying reduction and sometimes outright elimination of cost, the ancient model of organizing schools has persisted to modern times, with education costs and student debts now spiraling out of control.

One reason for this persistence may be that tenured professor jobs with six-figure salaries, excellent health insurance, and generous pensions are increasingly rare in the private sector. The academic priesthoods that benefit from the current system have a vast self-interest in perpetuating it no matter what. The ancient practices of oral lectures and costly texts are actively blocking lower cost superior methods. The organizational imperatives of this ancient system are clearly obsolete.

Why does the old style system still persist even though it is already demonstrably inferior? In addition to the financial disincentives, there is another reason: the current system retains a monopoly on assessing student learning and granting credit for demonstrated accomplishment. The schools are able to do this because they have arranged a monopoly on accreditation. This is ultimately a grant of state power.

As a result, modern colleges and universities have collectively become a rent-seeking cartel, an alliance of nominally competitive institutions that maintains a highly profitable monopoly of accreditation. To grasp the power of the cartel, consider a typical Physics I course even at MIT is almost entirely based on Newtonian mechanics, and the subject matter entirely in the public domain. Only a cartel could arrange to charge $1,500 and more per student for tuition and texts, in the face of far lower cost and superior quality materials, for subject matter that is no more recent than the 19th Century.

Breaking down this system means developing alternate methods to accredit what already exists. This is individual learning. Rather than accrediting institutions, the NFU must aim at accrediting individuals directly.

Part One:
The Nearly-Free University

Chapter 1: A New Model for Higher Education

We all have first-hand knowledge of school and learning, and most of us have navigated the world of work. Our experience may have made us an expert in how we learn and what kind of work best suits us, but it sheds little light on the systemic connections between education, learning and becoming productive in the fast-evolving *emerging economy*.

Economists use the phrase *emerging economies* to describe rapidly developing national economies. I use the term *emerging economy* to describe the digital-software-fabrication-robotics-automation (DSFRA) innovations that are rapidly transforming every sector of the global economy.

The U.S. economy has entered an era of profound technological transformation akin to the Industrial Revolution that remade America in the late 19th and early 20th centuries. New technologies transform more than just production of goods and services: they also change the social and political order, and the nature of work (labor) and capital. As a result, the assumptions and projections based on the previous era are no longer valid.

A phrase commonly attributed to Henry Ford captures the way technology invalidates projections based on the past era: If I'd asked people what they wanted, they'd have said faster horses.

This book explores the dynamic relationship between the economy and our system of higher learning. While the economy is being transformed in fundamental ways, our system of higher education remains essentially unchanged from the post-World War II industrial era—what I call *the factory model of education*.

No sector of the economy is immune to this technological transformation, and the higher education sector is bubbling with technology-enabled innovations such as massively open online courses (MOOCs) that distribute lectures once confined to a single classroom to millions of students' digital devices.

But these innovations in higher education are in essence aimed at breeding faster horses, that is, maintaining a status quo system of a bygone era that no longer serves the emerging economy. This widening divide between the emerging economy and higher education manifests in two ways: while the cost of higher education has skyrocketed (tuition is up 1,100% since 1980), the value of college education and diploma has declined. Indeed, one national study, *Academically Adrift*, found that over one third of college students "did not demonstrate any significant improvements in learning" critical thinking and other skills central to success in the emerging economy.

The era in which a college degree in almost any field virtually guaranteed a secure white-collar job has passed. There are many reasons for this, but the primary one is that the economy is changing at the most fundamental levels. The dominant features of the current post-industrial economy—financial capital and centralized institutions—have reached the terminal stage of their effectiveness. The critical features in the emerging economy are decentralization, adaptability, transparency and accountability (what I term the DATA model), and the essential assets are *human and social capital*.

If higher education is to effectively serve our society, we must understand these systemic connections between learning, knowledge and the emerging economy. To do that, we must understand the emerging economy in some detail and identify what is indispensable for students to become productive in this economy.

There are four basic levels in the current higher education system:

1. the two-year community college and vocational training system;

2. the four-year universities that issue bachelor's degrees;

3. the professional and graduate schools; and

4. the research universities, which receive federal funding to conduct a wide array of research, often in conjunction with government agencies, non-profit institutions and the national laboratories.

Though there are clear differences between each sector, higher education as a whole has a number of systemic characteristics.

Before we examine these traits, it's important to stipulate that the industry's failings are systemic, and do not reflect the positive intentions and efforts of those working in higher education, any more than the systemic failures of U.S. healthcare reflect the good intentions and efforts of those employed in that industry. Despite the good intentions and hard work of individuals, these systems are broken.

Due to their size and structure, large systems such as national defense, healthcare and education limit the impact of individual initiative. This has several consequences. One is that individuals feel powerless to change the system and so they relinquish responsibility for changing it. As Voltaire observed, "No snowflake in an avalanche ever feels responsible." A second consequence is psychological. Even if the system is visibly flawed or failing, insiders feel obligated to defend the system and their role in it, for two compelling reasons: self-preservation and the psychological need to believe in the value of one's place in the institution.

Answering the question *cui bono*, to whose benefit, illuminates the line between self-interest and claims of serving the public interest. Thus everyone participating in building an obsolete weapons system plagued by horrendous cost overruns will defend it as essential to national security, and those employed in the U.S. healthcare system will justify every dollar spent even though the system costs twice as much per person as healthcare in competing advanced democracies. Higher education is no different; those employed by the industry are compelled to minimize its failings and defend its standing as a secularly sacred industry.

Every institution defends itself against external analysis by marginalizing or discrediting those who could potentially limit its funding and power. Those few within the institution who reveal the systemic rot (whistleblowers) or attempt reforms that threaten the status quo are portrayed as troublemakers who must be neutralized or cast out for the good of the institution and all who work for it.

Applying this to the higher education system, we can anticipate that those employed by the higher education industry will deny that it is failing, and all the institutions within the system will devote tremendous resources to marginalizing or suppressing critics who find it obsolete, ineffective, unaffordable and unsustainable. These defensive responses are natural, but they don't help us assess whether higher education actually **is,** in fact, obsolete, ineffective, unaffordable and unsustainable, any more than the claims of defense contractors help us assess if their incredibly costly weapons systems are obsolete and unaffordable.

Let's start with what is self-evident about the basic structure of higher education:

1. As my colleague Mark Gallmeier noted in the *Foreword*, higher education is a legacy system based on the scarcity of recorded knowledge (printed and other media) and informed lectures. Both recorded knowledge and informed lectures are now essentially free and readily available. This is the material basis of the alternative system outlined in this book, the Nearly Free University (NFU), whose core is an *open-enrollment, universally accessible, individually accredited curriculum designed for the emerging economy and the individual student.*

2. The current higher education model is a factory composed of broadcast lectures and mass-distributed reading/coursework/tests. The student moves down the assembly line, attending the same lectures as other students, reading the same materials and taking the same tests. When the student receives a passing grade in a quasi-arbitrary number of courses, he or she is issued a diploma.

   This *factory model of education* is fundamentally unchanged from the era of World War II, when the government expanded higher education from its traditional elitist function to serve the nation's war production. While factories churned out war materiel with low-skill labor, behind the scenes the war effort demanded a vast increase in engineering and scientific skills. This began the transformation into a *knowledge-based economy*. The difference between an industrial economy that requires massive numbers of low-skill factory workers and a knowledge-based (often referred to a post-industrial) economy is the knowledge of its workers.

   The factory model is obsolete in an era where a variety of nearly-free instructional materials and methodologies enable the student to select the most appropriate approach for his aptitudes and needs.

3. In terms of its financial structure, higher education is a cartel-like system that limits its product (accredited instruction) and restricts its output (credentials, diplomas). (A cartel is an organization of nominally competing enterprises that fixes prices and production to benefit its members. Cartels may be formal, such as the Organization of Oil Exporting Nations (OPEC) or informal like the higher education cartel. Informal cartels often rely on government regulations to restrict competitors' entry into their market and on government spending or loans to fund their operations. To mask the uncompetitive nature of their cartel, they devote enormous resources to public relations.)

    The cartel's basic mechanism of maintaining non-competitive pricing is to enforce an *artificial scarcity of credentials*. The cartel's control of a product that is in high demand (college diploma) frees it from outside competition and free-market price discovery, enabling it to charge customers (students) an extraordinary premium for a product whose value is entirely scarcity-based.

    This is the very definition of a *rent-seeking cartel*, a cartel that extracts premiums solely on the basis of an artificial scarcity. By their very nature, rent-seeking cartels are exploitive and parasitic, drawing resources from those who can least afford to pay high premiums and misallocating capital that could have been invested in productive social investments. The term *rents* in this context means that the cartel collects a premium without providing any corresponding additional value. The *rentier class* includes landed aristocracy, who collect rents while adding no value to the production of their tenant farmers.

4. Since the higher education cartel is the sole provider of accreditation (college diplomas), it is unaccountable for its failure to prepare its customers (students) for productive employment in the emerging economy. If a diploma is portrayed as essential, students must pay the cartel even if the cartel's product (education) is ineffective and obsolete.

5. The four-year college system is profoundly disconnected from the economy. That the cartel's product has little practical application is not considered a factor in the value of the product (diploma), whose primary purpose is to act as a *higher education passport* that enables passage to a more expansive territory of employment.

6. The present system of higher education is unaffordable for all but the wealthy. The cartel's solution to its high prices, $1 trillion in student loan debt (exceeding both credit card debt and vehicle loans), is a crushing burden on both individuals and society at large.

7. The higher education cartel is an intrinsically elitist force, as its survival as a rent-seeking cartel is based on limiting what is now essentially free: knowledge and instruction. In other words, the higher education cartel charges an extraordinary premium for a free product.

8. The only way the Higher Education cartel can continue to charge a premium for nearly-free products is to actively *mystify its product* (by attributing secular sanctity and civic value to its diplomas) and *promote an artificial value for this product using public relations and political lobbying*. In other words, the higher education cartel operates on the same principles as other informal cartels: it depends on the state to fund its operations, and it uses public relations to mask its cartel structure and systemic failure to fulfill its original purpose.

The higher education cartel's dependence on federal funding and enforcement of student loans is readily visible in the Federal Reserve's Flow of Funds report, Table L.105, which shows the Federal Government's assets and liabilities. Direct Federal loans to students have exploded higher, from $93 billion in 2007 to $560 billion in early 2013. This gargantuan sum exceeds the gross domestic product (GDP) of entire nations—for example, Sweden ($538 billion) and Iran ($521 billion). Non-Federal student loans total another $500 billion, bringing the total to $1 trillion.

A variety of cultural traditions have effectively obscured these self-evident truths, even as the system's diminishing returns and rising costs have rendered it unsustainable.

The alternative is equally self-evident: knowledge and instruction should be nearly free, and students should be accredited directly, dissolving the monopoly on accreditation that gives higher education its cartel-like power to extract artificial premiums.

I am fully aware that this critique is exceedingly unwelcome to those whose livelihood depends on the higher education cartel. I am also aware that this critique upends most or all of the secularly sacred cultural traditions that the higher education system nurtures to justify its premium.

This is the key question: does the current higher education system exist to serve students, or does it exist to serve those employed by the system? Those with vested interests in the system will naturally answer "both," but to answer this question fairly, we must ask if an alternative system that accredits each student could serve students more effectively than current system of accrediting schools.

Let's imagine another system, one in which the Nearly Free University and the existing higher education cartel compete to prepare students for individual third-party accreditation of the critical skills and knowledge base needed to *establish and maintain a livelihood in the emerging economy*. If the Nearly Free University costs $4,000 for a four-year program (not including room and board) and the higher education cartel charges between ten and 25 times more for the same number of courses, then the higher education cartel had better be 25 times better at preparing students to establish and maintain a livelihood in the emerging economy, or it will lose its customers.

Limiting access to accreditation to skim enormous premiums based on scarcity is not just unethical; it is intellectually dishonest. Cartels are intrinsically extractive, exploitive and parasitic, and no amount of vested-interest justification changes this reality. Creating an artificial scarcity is financial manipulation, and all financial manipulation is ultimately a form of theft.

Progressives, by the very definition of their creed, must support the dissolution of all cartels. Those within the higher education system must choose between financial allegiance to their cartel or refusal to support cartels.

A cartel whose *raison d'etre* is to limit access to accreditation cannot possibly serve students; indeed, its very existence is a profound disservice to students and society. If we accredit the student, not the school, then the true value of every school will soon be established.

There may well be students who will choose to pay $140,000 for the privilege of an institutional association with a semi-professional sports team (a college team) and a large piece of real estate (a college campus), but the vast majority of those seeking an education with real-world applications will find considerably less than $140,000 of value in the *social/sports* aspects of higher education.

As for research universities: obtaining funding and conducting research is distinct from preparing undergraduate students to be productively employed in the real economy. Subsidizing a university's research and administrative costs with a cartel based on artificial scarcity and crushing student debt is a corruption of higher education's original purpose: a system that was supposed to serve students now serves itself.

Everything has a cost and a yield (return on investment). This is true even in a socialist economy. The only difference between a socialist economy and a market economy is the costs and yields are hidden in the socialist system, as are the subsidies diverted from productive sectors to support unproductive sectors.

Price and yield are the feedback that enables the economy to function efficiently and allow people to make rational decisions and investments. Once cartels distort or obscure price and yield, it becomes impossible to make informed investment decisions, and the resulting misallocations of risk, debt and capital cripple the economy.

What is the market value of instruction and accreditation? The feedback of price and yield does not exist in a cartel system.

The only way to enable price/yield discovery in higher education is to dissolve the accreditation monopoly and let a thousand flowers of innovation and transparency bloom: once we accredit the student rather than the school and base that accreditation on professional standards developed by those working in the real economy, the floodgates of useful cost and results feedback will open.

One purpose of this book to investigate *what can be learned and what must be taught*, and to use this investigation to design a truly effective curriculum designed around the needs of the individual student and real-world enterprises in the emerging economy.

The fundamental feature of the emerging economy actively depreciates the value of any credential, regardless of its origin: in a decentralizing economy, *what matters is what you can do, not what credential you hold*.

This raises the key question: what is the purpose of higher education?

What Is the Purpose of Higher Education?

What is the purpose of higher education, and is today's higher education industry effectively fulfilling that purpose? Given the astronomical rise in the cost of higher education and the resulting debt-serfdom of students burdened with over $1 trillion student loans, the discussion of higher education's purpose is far from academic.

The first question is actually three related inquiries:

What is the purpose of higher education?

What is the purpose of a college-level diploma or certificate?

What is the purpose of higher educational institutions?

I think it is self-evident that institutional education has four fundamental purposes:

1. To prepare the student to earn a livelihood
2. To prepare the student to work effectively in organizations and groups
3. To prepare the student to be a responsible citizen
4. To prepare the student to think critically and pursue lifelong learning and self-improvement

Basic socialization and civic skills (# 2 and #3) and learning how to learn (#4) are taught in primary and secondary schools. That leaves the sole purpose of higher education the preparation of students to *establish and maintain a livelihood in the emerging economy*.

As for the purpose of a diploma: it certifies that the student has systemically worked through a curriculum. In the current system, it certifies the student sat in a classroom for the specified number of hours, completed specified lab work and earned passing grades in the minimum number of courses. Since this accreditation methodology is intrinsically disconnected from real-world employers and markets, the diploma does not and indeed, cannot reflect the student's readiness for productive work in the emerging economy.

In the workplace, the current system's diplomas act as a stamp on the student's *higher education passport*, evidence of the student's perseverance and ability to navigate institutional processes, not his readiness for producing value in the real-world economy. Since the eight critical skills needed to successfully navigate the emerging economy (listed later in this chapter) are not on the curriculum, the existing higher education industry is incapable of preparing students to establish and maintain livelihoods in the emerging economy.

In terms of the economy and society at large, the purpose of higher education institutions is to prepare students for productive work in an economy that places a premium on creating value with human and social capital, which we will discuss in Chapter 2.

How Effectively Is Higher Education Fulfilling This Purpose?

I think my own experience serves as a relatively common example. The skills and knowledge I have employed to earn a living were not learned in a classroom, or indeed, any institution, despite my four-year university bachelor's degree. All my marketable skills and specialized knowledge were gained on my own, from either work experience or self-guided study.

This is an extraordinary statement, for it suggests an astonishing lack of real-world utility in higher education. This is not simply a financial failing for an enormous investment of time (four years) and money (between $85,000 and $170,000 for a bachelor's degree); it is a social failure as well, for everything I have learned about being an engaged, informed citizen was also learned outside institutional higher education.

Some might claim that this astonishing lack of real-world utility is unique to me, or the result of my liberal arts degree, or even to the era of my university study (1971-1975), but they would be wrong on all counts. The lack of real-world utility in terms of fashioning a livelihood is an intrinsic feature of the current system of higher education, whose substance and structure has changed very little over the past 60 years.

It continues to be what I term the *Factory Model of Education*; a post-World War II system that took an elitist structure of university education designed for 5% of the populace and expanded it with assembly line production efficiency to educate almost half of the workforce.

Only 5% of adults had a college degree in 1940. Today, over 50% of American adults have some college experience, 40% have a college diploma and over 25% have earned four-year college degrees.

Technology has not yet transformed the current higher-education model. Distributing lessons digitally via MOOCs is not a change in either substance or structure; it is simply adding another distribution channel of the existing curriculum, content and focus.

Conventional lectures and MOOCs can help students learn subject matter, but *learning skills requires doing.* We all understand this is true in the practical skills of cooking, carpentry, driving a vehicle, playing a musical instrument, etc. No amount of passively watching a lecture, either live or online, will teach a student how to cook, drive an auto, play guitar, build a cabinet or operate a digital fabrication device.

The only substantial change over the past forty years has been an alarming increase in cost. Tuition and other college costs are between four and ten times the inflation-adjusted totals of forty years ago. Various explanations have been offered for this unprecedented increase—decreasing state subsidies and higher healthcare costs, for example—but the point here is the utility of the education industry's output has declined as the economy has changed while the cost of higher education has skyrocketed. This is the very definition of diminishing returns.

Even more disturbing, this vast increase in cost is being paid with debt. That is an extraordinary change that receives little critical inquiry.

Various studies substantiate this decline in the returns on the increasingly costly investment in higher education. One national study that is available online, *Academically Adrift*, found that over one third of college students "did not demonstrate any significant improvements in learning" critical thinking and other skills central to success in the emerging economy.

The other substantial change over the past forty years has been the structural transformation of the U.S. economy. Not only has America transitioned from a largely industrial economy to a post-industrial service economy, the digital processing, fabrication and communications revolution is transforming the labor-intensive service economy into a knowledge-based economy with dramatically lower needs for human labor. The pace of change in this emerging economy demands adaptability and a high level of human and social capital of its participants.

As I write in mid-2013, the first sectors to experience this structural change include the newspaper, music, travel booking and publishing industries. Cartels and guilds in these sectors have been fatally disrupted as the emerging economy introduces transparency, decentralization, competition and lower costs to previously protected industries.

Government—what political economists call *the state*—has long played a central role in creating and protecting cartel-like structures. These cartels present a public-relations claim of competition and transparency that is entirely specious; behind the PR screen, supply is tightly controlled and prices maintained at high levels.

Sectors that exhibit cartel-like structures include national defense, healthcare and higher education. The emerging economy is just starting to undermine these protected industries.

That which is unsustainable will go away. This fundamental truth is the driver of the emerging economy. It is unsustainable to devote almost 20% of the national gross domestic product (GDP) to a diminishing-return system of healthcare, just as it is unsustainable to fund diminishing-return higher education with ever-increasing mountains of student debt.

Though those tasked with protecting the privileged income stream of the higher education sector will claim that their industry is indeed training students to be successful in the emerging economy, this is public relations rather than fact. The reality is that higher education as an industry has no idea how the emerging economy functions.

Expecting an industry—higher education—that has essentially no participation in the emerging economy to prepare people to navigate the emerging economy opens a profound disconnect. The only way higher education can effectively prepare people for the emerging economy is to become part of the emerging economy, and that requires dismantling the entire cartel-like structure of higher education. This means relinquishing control of the key product in the higher education supply-demand matrix—credentials—and opening the sector to everything it currently suppresses: accountability, transparency, decentralization and true competition.

To return to the initial point: if the college graduate must learn how to establish and maintain a livelihood and become an engaged citizen outside the institutions of higher learning, then clearly the hundreds of billions of dollars we are spending on higher education is yielding a poor return, and must be identified as a colossal misallocation of scarce capital.

Protecting the Higher Education Cartel

It is human nature to protect one's income stream by any means available. It is thus natural that we justify our claim on the national income in some compelling fashion, and this is the first line of public-relations defense of all the cartel-like structures in finance, national defense, healthcare and education. What is more sacrosanct than education, healthcare and national defense?

The propaganda method is to identify the sector's current structure as a given and to label any critical assessment of that structure as an unwarranted and dangerous attack on the *purpose of the sector*: providing national defense, education, healthcare, etc.

But the assessment isn't questioning the original purpose; it is investigating *how far the cartel structure has strayed from its original purpose* and whether the original purpose has been lost or subjugated to the *institutional pursuit of protecting the cartel and its income streams.*

As noted previously, the cartel's structure is intrinsically unaccountable, as abject failure to prepare students for real-world work and effectively accredit students' applicable knowledge and skills has not affected the cartel's prices, which continue to rise, or the demand for its product (diplomas).

Some argue that the deficiencies of the current system result from a lack of communication between employers and higher education; my point is the cartel has little incentive to engage employers or systemically measure the real-world effectiveness of its curriculum because neither the demand for its product (diplomas) nor the price it charges for the product are affected by failure.

The only dynamic that would make the current higher education system accountable is the introduction of a real competitor (The Nearly Free University) whose product (diplomas) are issued by organizations outside the cartel, for example, an accrediting body that accredits students individually based on their test scores and the successful completion of real-world projects.

All institutions adopt the same model to preserve their perquisites and power: subvert the state to protect their interests; devote enormous resources to public relations to elevate their claims on the national income to the sacrosanct pantheon of Mom and Apple Pie, untouchable to inquiry and accountability; relentlessly obscure evidence of self-service and diminishing returns; mask the cartel-like structure of their industry; make unsubstantiated claims about the value of their output; justify the ever-higher costs of maintaining their cartel's income and power as "essential;" undermine their critics and critical inquiries with all the usual propaganda techniques—Ad Hominem attacks that target the person rather than the arguments or evidence, presenting specious counter-examples, assemble cherry-picked data to support their effectiveness, etc.; suppress competition as "dangerous"; institute simulacrum reforms that only harden their control of supply and pricing; co-opt critics who cannot be marginalized or discredited, and defend their failure to serve their original purpose with high-minded appeals to this original purpose.

This sort of propaganda persuades the credulous and distracts those who should know better, but it doesn't make unsustainable systems sustainable. It simply puts off the day of reckoning, and increases the ultimate disruption of the cartels by the emerging economy.

Ironically, failure is a key justification for a cartel's expansion of income and power. As the health and well-being of Americans declines, the healthcare sector demands even more money to fix its own failure to focus on wellness rather than profiting from chronic disease and defensive medicine.

As the value of its output—education and credentials—decline, the higher education cartel demands more money to issue even more credentials as the solution to its failure to educate students to be effective in the emerging economy.

The Roots of the Factory Model

Traditionally, the university served two functions: as a repository of knowledge and scholarship and as a training facility for the social, political and economic Elite. Young men of the top social class attended university as a matter of course, and a smattering of lower-class individuals of great promise were admitted by way of meritocracy.

The university thus served several functions: it trained the next generation of scholars, it served as a finishing school for the sons of the Elite, and it educated the relative handful of scientists, engineers, military officers, doctors and lawyers needed by a largely agricultural, rural society.

In response to these three quite different purposes, the university system soon branched into specialty schools (medicine, law, military) and into two divisions: undergraduate for general education and a graduate doctoral level for training the next generation of scholars. The undergraduate level, populated by the offspring of the Elites, extended adolescence by four years and cultivated the *social capital* (social skills and connections) needed to marry well and move fluidly in the upper-class circles.

Practical skills had no place in the university system, as it was understood the practical aspects of life would be taken care of by lower-class workers and servants; the largest employment category at the turn of dawn of the 20th century was household domestics.

Non-Elites attended university for higher-level applied skills such as engineering. Management as we understand it today, as a profession dedicated to managing people and production, did not exist. The practical skills of metalworking, etc. were typically taught in apprenticeship programs whose roots extended back to medieval guilds and the artisan class.

Prior to World War II, only the top 5% of the populace had a university degree; this included a thin slice of doctors, lawyers, engineers, graduates of the military academies and scholars, and a larger cohort of Elite youths who had attended university as a finishing school for the upper class.

Those demanding more education for the general populace were not calling for universal higher education but improved high school courses and graduation rates.

America's industrial response to World War II was straightforward: existing factories were retooled to manufacture armaments, and new plants were quickly built to assemble hundreds of ships, thousands of aircraft and tens of thousands of vehicles.

Unlike previous wars, this war was global and required the entire nation's resources. It was also the first war that depended heavily on advanced engineering, technology and management. Producing stupendous numbers of armaments and moving them around the world required new advances in management, and the superiority of the Axis weaponry demanded new levels of engineering and applied research to compete and win on the battlefield.

The nation's tiny scientific Elite was enlisted to engineer rapid improvements in communications, encryption, code-breaking, weapons delivery and of course the super-bomb, the atomic bomb program that employed tens of thousands of researchers, technicians and managers.

The war effort transformed the American society and economy in a number of fundamental ways, one of which was the transformation into a knowledge-based industrial economy that required a vast number of engineers and managers to operate.

In response to this transformation, the small, elitist university system was rapidly expanded from a small-scale artisanal system to a factory model capable of churning out millions of graduates funded by Federal government spending on military research and development and the G.I. Bill, which gave veterans the financial wherewithal to attend university.

For the first time, the university system was open to the non-Elites classes. The expansion opened millions of slots for incoming students (including young women who had been recruited to work in the war effort) that effectively reduced the need for extreme filters of meritocracy. In essence, anyone who graduated from high school could find a college willing to accept them. Where it was extremely rare for a lower-class individual to attend college before the war, it became the norm to attend college for at least a year or two after the war.

It's important to recall that this was an era of typewritten orders, memos and invoices, and management of these new sprawling industries required a new army of managers as well as clerks, typists, and other office positions. The development of management led to the creation of business schools, but an old implicit assumption still held sway in society: anyone with a college degree was presumed to be qualified to manage and lead, regardless of their field of study, as anyone with a college education was considered superior, either by class or merit.

A rapidly expanding industrial economy—and after that phase, an equally dynamic post-industrial economy—had an insatiable appetite for specialists in engineering, materials science, communication, electronics, and of course teachers and professors for the expanding university system, and for generalists who could enter management, marketing and sales positions without any specialized, applied knowledge. (Sociologist Daniel Bell's book *The Coming Post-Industrial Society,* published in 1973, popularized the term *post-industrial.* The term denotes service/knowledge-based economies.)

Was the university system re-designed to serve this new economy? No, the existing elitist system was simply ramped up into a Factory Model, where lectures were given to hundreds of students instead of a dozen students, the same textbooks were printed in the tens of thousands instead of in the hundreds, and the same standardized tests were administered to millions instead of a few thousands.

Just as the U.S. economy ramped up to churn out tens of thousands of aircraft, vehicles and munitions, the university system took the template of the elitist institution and replicated it to move millions of students down an assembly line of higher education.

This expansion democratized the finishing-school features of undergraduate life: non-elite students could join sororities and fraternities, study abroad for a semester, and reap the social capital enrichment of the college experience. It also democratized social mobility: a university diploma enabled an individual to move from a lifetime prospect of being a worker to an upwardly-mobile manager, and from the working class to a higher social class whose primary signifier was the college degree. The school or subject was less important than the accreditation itself, which served as a passport to a new territory of opportunity.

We can now understand how the Factory Model arose in response to the industrialization of management and engineering in the postwar economy, and how its expansion seemed limitless: there were jobs for every PhD, regardless of the field of study, and jobs for everyone with an undergraduate degree, regardless of the school or field of study. It was presumed a general college education prepared the graduate to enter essentially any white-collar position as management material.

But just as the centralized, federally funded war-industrial economy gave way to the consumerist post-industrial economy, the post-industrial economy is giving way to the emerging economy. We will cover the emerging economy in later chapters, but the key point here is that a general education degree is no longer a passport to guaranteed white-collar employment, nor does a specialized doctorate degree guarantee a high-level position. The very fields that created the need for millions of college graduates—engineering and administration/management—have become automated just as assembly line industries have been automated.

This legacy system of mass-produced college diplomas, the Factory Model, made the transition from an industrial economy to a post-industrial economy in the 1960s and 70s because tens of millions of general-education graduates were absorbed into four expanding sectors: the financialization industry (the so-called FIRE economy of finance, insurance and real estate), the consumer-driven sectors of sales and marketing, the government funded fields of healthcare and education and the digital technology industries.

Those with PhDs found high-level jobs within academia itself, government or industry, depending on the field of study.

All of these industries have reached the point of saturation and diminishing returns: financialization has hollowed out the economy and triggered systemic instability; sales and marketing are being revolutionized by digital technologies; the enormous resources being poured into healthcare and education feed vested interests while yielding fewer measurable results, and the digital technologies are automating not just engineering and management in every sector but the very process of engineering advances.

The Factory Model of higher education has failed to make the transition to the emerging DSFRA economy, and indeed, cannot make the transition as it is structurally disconnected from this new economy. A general education no longer prepares students for work in the new economy, and there is no longer an insatiable need for ever greater numbers of PhDs in every field.

Legacy systems fail for a number of reasons, including loss of adaptability, higher costs coupled with diminishing returns, institutional sclerosis, vested interests incapable of reforming themselves out of a job, mission creep, loss of the original purpose, and so on. But the deeper reason is that the legacy system itself is the impediment to progress; as a result, even modest reforms trigger collapse of a system that has become obsolete.

One place to start an investigation of any legacy system is to ask: how would we design the system now from scratch? Would we take an elitist educational system from the 19th century and hoist a 20th century mass-production factory model on it? No, we would not; such an outdated, cumbersome system would be quickly rejected as counterproductive, overly costly and systemically ineffective.

The Four Higher Education Solutions of the Nearly Free University

There are four broad technology-enabled solutions would free higher education from its current cartel limitations on opportunities for structured learning and accreditation:

1. *Accredit the student, not the school.* This is my colleague Mark A. Gallmeier's succinct encapsulation of the key solution: by accrediting the student rather than the institution, we remove control of the credential supply and pricing from the cartel and establish the value of what the student has mastered by objective standards.

The concept of accrediting the student, not the school is well-established in the professions. Obtaining a law or architecture degree does not confer the right to practice those professions in the real world; one must demonstrate mastery of the subject and trade by passing a lengthy examination.

How difficult would it be to transfer this concept to all students in higher education? In the digital age, there is no technological or cost barrier to establishing a largely automated online procedure for taking exams and making the results available to prospective employers or collaborators. (Some fields may require a proctored exam; there are numerous models for accrediting the student via real-world tests.)

The threat this poses to the present higher education industry is mortal: if a school fails to adequately prepare students for participation in the real economy, as evidenced by exams and other objective measures of mastery, then the credential issued by that school becomes irrelevant.

2. *Structure learning such that it no longer depends on large physical campuses and costly administration.* Higher education has two claims of value: one, the issuance of credentials (diplomas), and

two, the claim that the product (instruction) can only be gained in a classroom setting overseen by a high-cost bureaucracy.

Limiting the supply of credentials and controlling the pricing of this limited supply is what makes higher education a classic cartel-like structure. If we accredit the student rather than the school, the value of the credential instantly falls to near-zero. The only value the school can offer is to adequately prepare the student for objective measures of mastery. The credential itself has lost its limited-supply value.

If learning is no longer tethered to large physical campuses and elaborate administration (except by tradition), the industry's second claim on pricing power is lost. If education can be structured and administered without an expensive physical campus and bureaucracy, then the cartel loses the only remaining basis for its control of pricing higher education.

Massively open online courses (MOOCs) are part of what Mark Gallmeier calls the *age of unlimited pedagogy*: instruction on a vast array of subjects are already available digitally and are accessible by anyone with an Internet connection. This vast library of lessons is expanding daily, and includes discrete instruction on everything from sewing a button to digital logic design.

Workshops and laboratories still require a physical space and equipment, but as we will cover in more detail later, few undergraduate labs and workshops require large campuses and complex administration. The cost of many types of desktop lab equipment is falling rapidly, and working labs may offer alternatives to on-campus facilities. Where better to learn real-world skills than in the workplace?

3. *Tailor the curriculum to the needs of the real-world emerging economy and the methods of learning to the individual student.*

    The value proposition in education is no longer the live lecturer who assigns the same material to hundreds of students or the administration of this factory model of educational production; it is the *assembly of nearly-free learning tools that fit the needs of the real emerging economy and the individual student*. Classes no longer need be scheduled and attended during working hours; digital courses are available 24 hours a day, 7 days a week year-round. This schedule enables students to work and complete coursework on flexible schedules; only workshops and labs would require fixed schedules.

4. *Eliminate the artificial scarcity of admissions and accreditation.* The higher education's pricing power is ultimately based on restricting the supply of admissions (i.e. access to credentials) and credentials. The Nearly Free University model eliminates this artificial scarcity and the Elite-controlled spoils system it creates. The Nearly Free University is open to all; it has no artificial scarcity, no spoils system and no Elites.

You've probably noticed that I toggle between present and future tense in describing the Nearly Free University model; this reflects the divide between the technological features of the model, which are already in use, and the structure of accrediting the student, which awaits future development and adoption. For simplicity's sake, I will use the present tense, as it describes a model that exists in the here and now even if the implementation of that model is still in the future.

The Pareto Distribution and Higher Education

I often turn to the Pareto Distribution (the so-called 80-20 rule) as an analytic aid.

In the early 20th century, Italian economist Vilfredo Pareto (1848 - 1923) observed that about 80% of the land in his region was owned by about 20% of the populace. He found that income, wealth and a variety of natural distributions followed this same distribution pattern.

The Pareto Distribution is not a natural law like gravity but a power law of probability distribution that projects probabilities and ranges, not exact numbers. For example, the top 25% of U.S. wage earners pay 87% of the Federal income taxes. The point is not precision but the basic distribution.

The Pareto principle suggests that 80% of the effects arise from 20% of the causes. Thus changing 20% of the organizational structure of higher education will likely cause 80% of the effects.

We can project that these two solutions—accrediting the student, not the school, and structuring nearly-free learning tools to fit the economy and individual student—would eliminate the pricing power of perhaps

80% of all colleges and reduce the costs of a college-level education by 80%.

The Pareto Distribution rule can be further extended to a 64-4 rule (80% of 80 is 64 and 20% of 20 is 4): the power to instigate systemic change accrues to the 4% "vital few" who exert outsized influence on the "trivial many" 64%.

The 64-4 distribution is visible in a variety of settings. For example, the top 5% of American households control about 70% of all household assets. This is remarkably close to the 64-4 distribution predicted by the Pareto principle.

We can extend these distributions in a number of ways. It is possible that 4% of students participating in emerging-economy programs could trigger a transformation that affects 64% of all higher education students.

This distribution further suggests that perhaps 4% of all college instructors will originate the vast majority of massively open online courses (MOOCs) and shorter, targeted lessons that students, teachers and industry select as the most effective available. This consequence will be welcomed by students everywhere, who will finally have access to the very best instructors in the English-speaking world for near-zero cost.

As impossible as it seems to those who have been immune to the emerging economy, this also suggests costs could fall to levels that approach free—hence the title of this book, *the Nearly Free University*. If a conventional four-year bachelor's degree currently costs about $100,000 (not including room and board and wages lost to completing coursework), then the first-order Pareto principle suggests costs could fall by 80% to $20,000. But a second-order Pareto distribution suggests costs could fall from $100,000 to $4,000, or about $1,000 for the equivalent of ten courses per year.

Labs and workshops that require expensive materials and equipment will naturally cost more than MOOCs, but the digital-fabrication revolution is also transforming many lab settings: some equipment that once cost tens of thousands of dollars can now be purchased for a few hundred dollars, further eroding the premium placed on campus laboratories and widening the opportunities for those excluded from these institutionally controlled facilities.

Those fields of study that require experience in irreplaceably costly research university labs educate a relatively limited set of students, and even in these fields, the costs of lab time should be priced on a per-hour basis. In all cases, the question of alternatives must be thoroughly explored. Are there no equivalent labs in private industry that might be open to occasional use by mentors and students?

It is important to recall our original question: if we were to start afresh, are there any lower-cost alternatives to the present high-cost system? How can we assume the answer is "no" if the question is never fairly explored?

Another way to stimulate new thinking this is to ask, "How much effective student lab work could be arranged for $1,000 if that was all the money that was available?" If money is unlimited (for example, student loans), creativity is unnecessary.

We can anticipate that perhaps as few as the top 4% of universities— the large federal and state-funded research universities connected to national laboratories or equivalent research nodes—will retain a claim to value at the graduate and post-graduate levels. Since there are about 4,000 colleges in the U.S. (both four-year and two-year), that implies perhaps 160 research universities will retain their conventional structure. If we take the smaller subset of four-year universities (roughly 2,350) as the more accurate starting point, this implies that as few as 100 major universities will retain their conventional structure at the graduate and post-doctoral levels.

Given the possibilities that at least some of the expense and learning at these levels can be digitized, it may well be that even the traditional bastions of graduate-level research will not be immune to transformation.

Students vs. the Higher Education Cartel

The context of this discussion is very simple: is higher education for the students or is it for those benefitting from the cartel-like structure of the higher education industry? If we answer "it's for the students," then we must welcome the transformation of the industry and its integration into the emerging economy.

But the conflict between those benefitting from the cartel-like structure and students who would benefit from a radically lower cost alternative that accredits individuals rather than institutions is far from equal. On the surface, the higher education cartel has all the power and the students have only a no-win choice: either indenture oneself to student debt-serfdom or renounce the higher education system and risk the consequences of not having your *higher education passport* properly stamped.

But beneath the surface, two dynamics favor the students. One is the simple truth that what is unsustainable will go away; piling $1 trillion of debt onto students for an education that fails to prepare them for the emerging economy is neither ethical nor sustainable.

The other is that technology and innovation cannot be resisted for long, even by protected cartels with tremendous political power and vast propaganda machines. Once faster, better, cheaper solutions are available on the margins, those adopting the new solutions soon reach the critical 4% threshold and very quickly the vital 4% will revolutionize the experience of the 64% and then the 80%.

The adoption of the Internet itself is an example of this dynamic.

If we read between the lines of the many articles and books addressing higher education, it seems clear that the university-educated class holds an implicit assumption that its privileged status confers economic immunity to revolutionary reductions in labor and cost. This assumption is largely based on a scarcity that no longer exists. In the post-World War II decades of rapid expansion, those holding a four-year college degree were a relatively small percentage of the working-age population. In a rapidly expanding economy that increasingly demanded higher skills, this scarcity drove both the wages of the college-educated and the premium of a college education higher.

In this golden age of growth, any college degree granted access to higher paying jobs and advancement. This led to what I call the *higher education passport*, the notion that getting a college degree (i.e. having your higher education passport stamped) was the key to opening doors to advancement and higher earnings. The college that issued the degree and the field of study were not critical except in the Ivy League Aristocracy and for those few (2% of the populace) who went on to obtain doctorates (PhDs) or professional degrees in law and medicine.

This scarcity has diminished for three reasons:

1. One, the number of people with college degrees has ballooned to roughly 40% of the workforce. According to 2012 U.S. Census Bureau data, over 19 million adults have earned a two-year degree and over 39 million hold four-year degrees. Of these, 22 million have additional advanced degrees—masters, professional or doctoral. This means about 26% of the American workforce of 150 million has a four-year degree, and 15% have advanced degrees. Almost 40% of the workforce has a stamp on their higher-education passports, and millions more have some college experience.

2. The second reason is that digital technology has advanced to the point that it is not just automating low-skill labor but higher-skilled knowledge labor as well. To take but one example of many, tax preparation for the average household and sole proprietor, though certainly complex, no longer requires an accountant; software that costs less than $100 efficiently guides neophytes through the steps, and audit insurance, i.e. access to human expertise, is available for less than $50.

3. The third reason is saturation. In the era of rapid expansion, it was widely assumed that growth would continue on the same trajectory forever, and so the demand for engineers, doctors, attorneys, marketing professionals, designers and all the other white-collar fields would expand forever. But the economy's need for labor in white-collar fields has limits; graduating 100,000 attorneys and 100,000 chemists, for example, does not magically create demand for 100,000 additional attorneys or chemists. The expanding economy created the illusion that demand for specific expertise would expand forever, but the reality is that each field can only support a limited number of participants.

As long as the economy was expanding smartly, any downturn in demand for college-educated labor was presumed to be temporary and easily remedied by transferring to a related field. The unemployed chemist, for example, might take a job in marketing products to the chemical industry.

This presumption was valid as long as the scarcity of college degrees existed and the demand for skilled white-collar labor was expanding. But once those conditions changed, the presumption became invalid.

The unstoppable advance of technology and innovation is now reducing demand for white-collar labor and lowering wages paid for service-sector labor. As the competitive pressures of globalization and the cost of benefits such as healthcare rise, employers have powerful incentives to increase the productivity of workers and lower labor costs. Profitability in a slow-growth economy increasingly depends on lowering costs, and since labor is typically the largest component of cost, reducing the number of employees, the hours they are paid to work and their wages and benefits is the only path to maintaining profitability.

The higher education industry has responded to this surplus of associate's and bachelor's degrees and the saturation of the labor market by promoting another stamp on the higher education passport—a graduate or professional degree. However, since issuing additional stamps does not magically create more jobs, this inflation of certification has only served to provide employers with additional reasons to eliminate prospective employees from the crowd of applicants. (Being over-qualified offers one example.) And if there is little demand for newly-minted architects, for example, then the value of obtaining a master's degree in architecture may be lower than the value of obtaining real-world design experience.

This promotion of the idea that additional stamps on one's higher education passport translate into a competitive advantage in the job market has two pernicious consequences: it actively depreciates the value of the four-year bachelor's degree and moves the saturation point higher up the education food chain, creating systemic surpluses of those holding master's degrees and doctorates.

A debate rages within academia over the extent of the surplus of PhDs. Those supporting the status quo cite studies that find the unemployment rate among PhDs to be very low, while skeptics point out these studies do not adequately account for the critical difference between underemployment (i.e. a PhD working in a position that doesn't require a PhD) and unemployment. Anecdotally, there is evidence that the applicant with a PhD has simply displaced the candidate with the master's degree who previously displaced the applicant with the bachelor's degree.

While this inflation of higher education stamps reaps billions of borrowed dollars for the higher education cartel, the actual skills needed to prosper in the emerging economy go unrecognized and untaught.

The Eight Necessary Skills

This is perhaps the greatest blind spot in the higher education industry: the absolutely essential skills going forward are currently assumed to be transferred to college students by osmosis or magic rather than direct instruction.

What do I mean by osmosis or magic? *Critical skills are not taught directly, they are assumed to be transferred via standard coursework.* For example, *self-learning to mastery* is one of the essential skills needed to thrive in the emerging economy (skills 1 and 2 below). The current system assumes that following a curriculum imparts the specific skillset needed to learn on one's own to the point of mastery, but the ability to self-learn to mastery must be explicitly taught and learned.

The current system assumes that the interactions in classrooms and workshops impart the interpersonal skills needed to work effectively with others in the workplace, but this is also an assumption: it is quite possible to earn high marks in higher education and exit the system with poor interpersonal skills.

It is assumed that successfully navigating the institutional processes of higher education will impart professional working skills: showing up on time, performing as promised, being accountable, and so on. Once again, this assumption is false: *performing well in institutions of higher learning has no correlation to performance in the workplace.* This is the conclusion that Google reached after crunching reams of data.

Lazlo Bock, senior vice president of people operations at Google, made the following comments in an interview published by the *New York Times* in June 2013:

> *"One of the things we've seen from all our data crunching is that G.P.A.'s (grade point averages) are worthless as a criteria for hiring, and test scores are worthless. Google famously used to ask everyone for a transcript and G.P.A.'s and test scores, but we don't anymore.... We found that they don't predict anything.*

> *What's interesting is the proportion of people without any college education at Google has increased over time as well. So we have teams where you have 14 percent of the team made up of people who've never gone to college."*

Doing well in college—earning high test scores and grades—has no measurable correlation with being an effective worker or manager. This is incontrovertible evidence that the entire higher education system is detached from the real economy: excelling in higher education has no discernible correlation to real-world skills or performance.

If the higher education system does not explicitly teach these skills, students will not learn them, even if they excel in fulfilling the criteria of higher education.

The unspoken assumption of the current higher education system is "we're not a trade school; it's up to employers to teach their new employees." This is yet more evidence that higher education is completely out of touch with the real-world economy: in the real world, employers want new employees who are able to *profitably solve problems* on Day One.

The ultimate purpose of skills is to *profitably solve problems*. Problem-solving has become a cliché of sorts, and so we need to ask, what set of skills is required to profitably solve problems?

The set of necessary skills divides into two categories: *hard skills* in specific technologies and crafts and *soft skills* that enable *ownership of tasks and projects*, systematic application of creativity and critical thinking, and professional standards of collaboration and conduct.

These two sets of skills are essential parts of *human and social capital*, which we will explore in Chapter 2. The ultimate purpose of education is to learn how to acquire human and social capital, and the ultimate purpose of human and social capital is mastery of the skills needed to profitably solve problems.

Problem-solving and *accountability* have been generalized to the point that we need to specify what they actually mean. In my terminology, they mean taking ownership of tasks and projects, i.e. accepting sole responsibility in the same manner as an owner.

Hard skills in the STEM subjects (science, technology, engineering and math) are no longer enough: professional collaboration skills are increasingly essential even in workplaces that demand engineering and scientific proficiency. The *soft skills* of collaboration, adaptability, creativity, entrepreneurism and professional accountability are core skills in every sector of the emerging economy.

Soft skills are not learned by osmosis or magic; they must be taught as systematically as hard skills.

The skills needed to establish and maintain a livelihood in the emerging economy are the abilities to:

1. Learn challenging new material over one's entire productive life
2. Creatively apply newly-mastered knowledge and skills to a variety of fields
3. Be adaptable in all work environments
4. Apply a full spectrum of entrepreneurial skills to any task
5. Work collaboratively and effectively with others, both in person and remotely
6. Be professional, responsible and accountable in all work environments
7. Continually build human and social capital
8. Possess a practical working knowledge of financial and project management

If we step back and consider the abilities needed to succeed in the emerging economy, we marvel that anyone believes the prevailing (but unspoken) assumption that coursework in the conventional fields of language, history, science and the humanities magically instills these essential skills in students who absorb and regurgitate factory-model coursework.

If one of the tasks of higher education is to enable productive entry into the workforce, its inability to grasp the nature of the emerging economy and teach the skills that students must have to be effective in this economy means the industry has failed its core purpose.

Massively Open Online Courses (MOOCs) and Accreditation

The higher education industry's response to digital innovations such as MOOCs is to offer programs that are nearly free to deliver (MOOCs) and charge students thousands of dollars for the program's certificate, even though the students' access to the physical campus, research labs and tenured professors—the high-cost structure of the university—is essentially zero.

This "innovation" is the acme of the cartel structure: the cost of production can be near-zero but the cost to the consumer is kept high via artificial scarcity to keep profit margins fat and bureaucracies well-funded.

But does this supposed innovation—replacing a high-priced campus-based structure of coursework with a discounted-price series of massively open online courses—actually address the intrinsic weaknesses in the higher education industry? I believe it self-evident that it does not.

The critical skills listed above and actual mastery of productive knowledge both require *a curriculum designed for the emerging economy and the individual student* and collaborative workshop or laboratory settings. Substituting a series of factory-model MOOCs for a series of factory-model classes on campus is not an improvement; it is simply a higher-profit channel for distributing the same failed product.

As noted earlier, one purpose of this book to investigate *what can be learned and what must be taught*, and to use this investigation to design a truly effective curriculum designed around the needs of the individual student and real-world enterprises in the emerging economy. This curriculum combines the most effective digitally distributed instruction with real-world collaborative workshops and labs.

There is another unspoken systemic failure intrinsic to the higher education industry: to maintain its premium, the industry must limit access to the higher education passport stamp. If everyone in the nation had access to the same coursework and accreditation system, there would be no artificial limitation on the number of people who could earn college-level accreditation. As noted earlier, the higher education industry's preferred solution is to offer everyone a course of MOOCs and charge a fat premium for the certificate. Once we accredit the student, not the school, this premium goes away, and the cost drops from the equivalent of a house to the equivalent of a used auto in the Nearly Free University model.

That the existing system indentures students to decades of debt is of no concern to the higher education cartel, which actively supports higher debt levels and subsidies of that debt to fund its own ever-higher costs.

The social cost of the cartel's limiting access to higher education as a means of maintaining its income is incalculably high. If the cartel is willing to issue degrees online for a price, then we have to ask: what feature of MOOCs ties them to the cartel, other than the cartel's power to issue degrees?

The answer is that there is nothing about MOOCs that ties them the cartel except the system of accrediting schools rather than accrediting students directly. This made sense in the factory model of education which was designed to process students and stamp their paperwork as they moved down the assembly line to graduation and delivery to the workforce. But this system actively impedes the social goal of universally accessible education and mastery of economically useful knowledge and skills.

To clarify this process for those unfamiliar with accreditation: six regional associations accredit public and private colleges and universities in the U.S. Once a college is accredited, the degrees it issues to students have the gravitas of accreditation. The knowledge and skills of the student are not directly measured; the accredited college issues a degree based on student receiving a passing grade in the requisite courses.

That this opens the door to wildly different levels of actual student attainment is self-evident. (Recall that *Academically Adrift* found a third of all graduating college students failed to gain critical-thinking skills in their four long years of study.) Clearly, a system that measured the attainment of each student directly would be far more useful to future employers than the present system, whose failings are masked by the essentially meaningless accreditation-of-schools process.

Contrast this with professional licensing accreditation that directly measures student attainment. Which is superior? Clearly, the system that measures the attainment of each individual and accredits them based on their verifiable knowledge and skills. Why do we tolerate a system in which accreditation offers no transparent, verifiable baseline of attainment?

Suppose a structured series of lectures and workshops equivalent to the coursework in law school were available online for near-zero cost. If students who completed the course were able to pass a state bar exam and be licensed to practice law, then what is the purpose of accrediting a law school other than to grant it cartel status, i.e. charge exorbitant sums for artificial scarcity? A law degree is not the equivalent of a license to practice law for a critically important reason: the only way to verify that the student knows enough to competently practice law is to accredit the student directly.

Current Contributors to the Increasing Cost of Higher Education

Recall that college tuition has risen 1,100% in the past 30 years, after adjusting for inflation. (The $230 annual in-state tuition and fees I paid my alma mater the University of Hawaii-Manoa, adjusted for the 434% inflationary increase since 1975, would total $1,000 in 2013 dollars. The current tuition/fee cost is $9,400, an inflation-adjusted rise of 940%.)

What is driving the skyrocketing cost of higher education? Stripped of rationalizations, the answer is that as long as funding is essentially unlimited, costs will continue to rise. This is as true of higher education as it is of the Pentagon. In the current system, there are no real limits on student loans and government grants, and so there is no pressure on costs: universities raise prices, and students borrow more money to pay the higher fees.

This dynamic is clearly visible in the rising costs of administration, which have risen far faster than the cost of classroom instruction.

Some of these administration costs arise from processing and managing the immense system of student loans. In the Nearly Free University model, costs will be reduced to the point that there is no longer any need or justification for student loans. There is no longer any need to "go away to college" for the vast majority of the urbanized population and the fees will be so modest they can be paid in cash or subsidized by charities, churches, foundations, etc.

Students will still need to pay for food and a roof over their head, but the immense flexibility of the Nearly Free University model opens up more opportunities for earning while learning. Given that in the majority of households students aren't adding much additional cost by living at home, and the low cost of unprocessed (real) bulk food in America, room and board at home are typically significantly less expensive than dormitory living elsewhere. (Learning how to cook to lower costs is a skill that will pay lifelong dividends.)

This elimination of the debt-serfdom of student loans not only frees students of crushing debt, it also lowers the cost of higher education by eliminating one entire layer of administration.

This same dynamic will sweep through the rest of the administrative structure of the higher education industry. The key administrative tasks of enrollment, payment, monitoring test results and issuing accreditation can be automated online.

This wholesale destruction of a cartel's premium and labor force is not unprecedented; indeed, it is welcomed by everyone who is no longer forced to pay a premium for diminishing returns.

Though it breaks a taboo against discussing class in America, we should note that the highly educated shed few tears (or publicly squeezed out a few crocodile tears) for the millions of less-educated workers who lost jobs as technology reduced the need for human labor in blue-collar industries; the top 5% was as delighted as any other class to pay less for steel, autos, airfare, music and all the other industries whose workforces have been gutted by digital technologies, automation and robotics.

This destruction of livelihoods by "faster, better, cheaper" was considered the natural order of things when it was limited to blue-collar sectors, but now that it is about to dismantle the entire higher education industry, it is unethical, dangerous, etc. This is course the summit of hypocrisy. Technological innovation makes no class distinctions, and PhDs and MBAs can be displaced as readily as line assembly workers.

Now the bastions of the highly educated class, long presumed to be impervious to the forces of creative destruction, are about to experience the same radical reduction of labor and wages others have already experienced. Objective observers can discern the shock and fear of those who were convinced of their own immunity: after all, aren't things fine as they are? The hundreds of thousands of steel and auto workers who lost their livelihoods in the 1970s and 80s felt the same way, of course: why can't institutions and processes that have lasted for decades continue on unchanged?

As technology has advanced up the skills ladder, the knowledge and service-based industries that most people thought were permanent have been disrupted. For example, many observers bemoan the decline of the newspaper industry, but nostalgia and tradition are not enough to support an industry undercut by the Internet and the digital communications revolution.

The same can be said of the music industry, travel booking, publishing and a host of other knowledge/service industries in the front of the queue of digital disruption. We can bemoan the loss of things as they were, but the number of people willing to pay a high premium for legacy systems when lower-cost alternative are available is vanishingly small.

The number of those welcoming the wholesale elimination of their high-paying job (supported by cartel pricing) is as small as the number of people willing to pay the hefty premiums of cartel pricing once faster, better, cheaper alternatives become available.

The Limits of Predicting Emerging Trends

In discussing legacy systems such as the factory model of education and new technologies such as MOOCs, it is important that we recognize the limits on predicting the course of emerging trends.

Many of the emerging trends discussed in this chapter are already in operation, albeit on the margins. Georgia Tech, for example, has introduced what some are calling a *MOOC 2.0* master's degree in computer science that combines online courses with limited human tutoring and supervision for $6,600 (2013 dollars), an 85% reduction from the out-of-state tuition of $45,000 for the same degree earned on campus and a 70% reduction from in-state tuition of $21,000.

Other universities are experimenting with crediting students' proven competencies in addition to classroom time and in-class tests. Many colleges are already offering fully online undergraduate and graduate degrees, though anecdotal evidence in this fast-evolving field suggests the typical fees for an undergraduate bachelor's degree are a still-costly $40,000.

Many experiments in blended learning—incorporating digital learning tools into the classroom—are also underway in public and private colleges.

In the context of a cartel maintaining an artificial scarcity to justify high costs, these online programs within the legacy system of higher education are attempts to co-opt and control innovations that threaten the cartel's pricing power. Once in the public domain, however, innovation cannot be safely confined by cartel moats; it jumps the moat despite the best efforts of those seeking to protect their artificial-scarcity premiums.

Private online educational enterprises such as Coursera are offering their courses for free and issuing credentials (termed verified certificates) for fees of around $100 to $190 per course. Other online educational enterprises such as Saylor.org have a mission goal of offering high-quality courses and testing for near-zero fees.

This ferment of experimentation in both legacy universities and new digital-education enterprises makes it difficult to select the proper verb tense: do we use the present tense to reflect that these concepts are already manifesting in real programs, or do we use the future tense to reflect that these innovations are far from ubiquitous, and many won't make the transition to widespread use?

Despite the limitations on predicting the course of fast-evolving and innovating systems, I think the following dynamics will continue to apply:

1. Digital technologies and other innovations are broadening the higher education spectrum of costs and curriculum. The range of costs and courses that are available is broadening by the month. This is a positive development for higher education, students and employers/industry and thus for the economy and society at large.

2. The momentum of innovation and the burden of unsustainable costs will transform the present system of higher education, whether we approve of the process and the eventual result or not. Attempting to conserve what is failing and unsustainable simply forces the system to self-prune via the messy collapse of obsolete and diminishing-return systems.

    In other words, the higher education cartel is being dismantled not by critics but by fundamental forces that are deaf to our approval or opprobrium.

3. The superiority of accrediting the student rather than the school is self-evident. As education innovator Salman Khan observed in the August 2013 edition of *Scientific American*, we can now "decouple credentials from learning—today both these functions are done by the same institutions. This approach will allow anyone to prove that they have mastered a set of skills at a high level, whether they learned them on the job, at a physical school, through an online resource, or most likely, all of the above."

4. Artificial intelligence and so-called *big data* analysis will enable low-cost individual guidance of students to monitor their progress and adjust the pace and style of learning to each individual.

5. Those elements of educational innovation that are evolving to serve the core needs of the emerging economy will follow a Pareto Distribution path to ubiquity and widespread acceptance, while those that attempt to preserve the artificial-scarcity premiums of the legacy factory-model cartel will wither.

6. Collaboration across sectors and the sharing of what works and what doesn't will continue to expand, speeding the evolution and adoption of innovations in higher education.

7. Nobel laureate Herbert Simon (Economic Sciences, 1978) summarized the key characteristic of learning (which I will explore in Chapter 2): "Learning results from what the student does and thinks and only from what the student does and thinks."

Key concepts covered in this chapter:

- *Factory Model of Education*

- *Emerging economy*

- *The skills needed to establish and maintain a livelihood in the emerging economy*

- *How far has the cartel structure strayed from its original purpose in pursuit of protecting the cartel's income streams?*

- *Accredit the student, not the school*

- *Structure learning such that it no longer depends on costly campuses and administration*

- *Tailor the curriculum to the needs of the emerging economy and the methods of learning to the individual student*

- *Age of unlimited pedagogy*

- *The Nearly Free University*

- *Higher education passport*

Chapter 2: Work, Learning and Mastery

In Chapter 1 we identified the sole purpose of higher education: to prepare students to *establish and maintain a livelihood in the emerging economy*, which we defined as the *digital-software-fabrication-robotics-automation (DSFRA)* economy. We also identified four systemic solutions and the eight essential skills students need to master to thrive in the emerging economy.

In this chapter, we'll explore learning, creating economic value via work, and accreditation in the context of the emerging economy, as that is the real-world context of all higher education.

Before we begin, we need to establish the context for the discussion of work and learning. In the current model of higher education, college provides a general education. It is implicitly assumed that teaching actual work skills are the responsibility of the students' future employers. In other words, the assumption is that both undergraduate and graduate students will be hired on the basis of their field of study and their success in absorbing and regurgitating course content as reflected by their grade point average (G.P.A.). A lack of real-world skills is not considered a detriment, as it is assumed the employers will spend months training their new hires to actually be productive in the workplace.

This model no longer aligns with reality. Few employers are prepared to train new employees for more than a few days, and those with multi-month formal training programs for new hires tend to be extremely competitive professional enclaves such as investment banks and multinational law firms. This sea-change has a number of causes, including a surplus of college graduates, higher rate of employee turnover and rising competitive pressures to lower employee training costs. For many firms, it is cheaper and less risky to poach an experienced employee from a competitor than invest months and thousands of dollars training a new hire who may quit and join a competitor the moment their training is complete.

Even a PhD is no guarantee that the student is ready to be a productive employee; the doctoral graduates must spend additional years in post-doctoral positions in real-world work places to actually learn how to create real economic value.

The current higher education model does not serve students or employers; squandering four or more years on general knowledge that can be learned from online courses is a tremendous misallocation of time and capital.

The Nearly Free University (NFU) model is designed not just to dramatically lower the price of higher education, but just as importantly, it is designed to prepare students to enter the workforce fully trained in the skills that create economic value.

The current higher education cartel's reliance on employers to do the heavy lifting is obsolete in another key way. The entire world of work is changing in the emerging economy, and many people entering the workforce will work in new ways that lack paternalistic employers and conventional 40-hour work weeks. In the collaborative work model, each worker chooses to join a work group that is formed to complete a specific project. Once the project is finished, the group disperses and each individual selects a new project. Digital technologies not only enable this model of self-organizing, networked employment, they make this model much more efficient than hierarchical, centralized models.

Higher education must enable students to take a job the day after graduation and start creating economic value that same day. They must have mastered the eight essential skills by doing, not watching, and assembled enough human and social capital to learn whatever hard skills are required on their own.

If higher education cannot do this, it has failed the students, the emerging economy, and the nation. In contrast to the obsolete higher education cartel, the Nearly Free University views work and mastery of these essential skills as the two strands of education's DNA.

Seven Questions

To design the Nearly Free University model to serve the broadest possible audience for the lowest possible cost, we need to answer seven questions. The first two were posed in Chapter 1:

1. Is higher education for the students or is it for those benefitting from the cartel-like structure of the higher education industry?

2. What can be learned and what must be taught?

3. What types of work create economic value in the emerging economy?

4. How can higher education prepare students to do this work?

5. What skills are essential to creating economic value?

6. What is absolutely indispensable in the process of acquiring these skills?

7. What are the fundamental characteristics of the emerging economy?

Our answer to the first question was "the students." The cartel-like structure of higher education must be dismantled to serve the widest possible population of students at the lowest possible cost, with the goal of preparing students for productive participation in the emerging economy.

We define productive participation as *creating economic value*. The ability to create economic value enables students to *establish and maintain a livelihood in the emerging economy*, which is the sole purpose and goal of higher education.

To understand the interconnectedness of work, skills and learning, we must start by understanding *human and social capital*. Following that, we'll investigate the nature of work and the process of learning, exploring what can be learned via self-guided learning and what must be taught, i.e. learning by doing under the guidance of a master/mentor.

Since the ultimate goal of learning economically valuable skills is *mastery*, we must understand the experience and attainment of mastery.

The fundamental characteristics of the emerging economy (question #7 above) will be addressed in Chapter 3.

Understanding Human and Social Capital

Human capital is an inexact term for labor's ability to take financial (money and credit) and physical capital (tools) and create economic value. *Social capital* is the value derived from connections to others: the sum of friends, contacts, alliances, group memberships and networks that create *reciprocal sources of value*. The key word here is *reciprocal*, as social capital is a two-way dynamic: it isn't created by entitlement but by providing value to others, as well as deriving value from your association with them. Reciprocity is the heart of social capital.

Within the general spectrum of human and social capital there are more subtle forms of non-material/non-financial capital, what French sociologist Pierre Bourdieu termed *cultural and symbolic capital*.

One way to give the terms more precision is to consider the example of building a house: imagine that all the necessary tools and materials are laid out on the building site, and there is a bank account with sufficient money or credit to fund the complete construction.

Now we bring in a person with zero building experience and ask them to use the money, tools and materials to build the house solely on their own. Clearly, they will be unable to build the house because they lack the necessary *hard skills* of the building trades. They do not have the *human capital* needed to construct the house and create economic value out of the financial and material capital.

Without human capital, the financial and material capital is *dead money*. It is incapable of generating value, profit or wealth.

Suppose we enable the person to use their *soft skills* to organize others to build the house. The eight essential skills listed in Chapter 1 are the core soft skills, the positive values and range of skills we might term professionalism: being able to communicate effectively, take responsibility, be accountable, etc. Here is the list again:

1. Learn challenging new material over one's entire productive life

2. Creatively apply newly mastered knowledge and skills to a variety of fields

3. Able to set goals and be adaptable in all work environments

4. Apply a full spectrum of entrepreneurial skills to any task
5. Work collaboratively and effectively with others, both in person and remotely
6. Be professional, responsible and accountable in all work environments
7. Continually build human and social capital
8. Possess practical working knowledge of financial and project management

If the person lacking hard skills in building has abundant soft skills, they should be able to recruit and manage others to build the house.

This illustrates why these eight skillsets are essential: they enable anyone who owns these skills as part of their human capital to create economic value, even if they lack the applicable hard skills at the start of a project.

It is vital that we understand that these soft skills are the foundation for hard skills: if one has the eight essential soft skills, one can learn hard skills. However, note that this does not work in reverse: having hard skills does not give a person the tools to acquire soft skills.

To understand *social capital*, let's imagine two scenarios.

1. In the first case, the person tasked with building the house is given the site, financial capital and building materials in an unfamiliar locale where he knows no one; he is a complete stranger. He has no friends, contacts, alliances, group memberships or networks—he owns no social capital at all.

   It's like arriving in a city and not knowing a single person.

2. In the second scenario, the inexperienced builder is given the task in his home community, where he has friends, contacts, alliances, group memberships and networks. Even if he doesn't know a single tradesperson or subcontractor, he can quickly utilize his social capital to identify trustworthy craftspeople to help him build the house.

This is like arriving in a strange city but knowing a few well-connected people: suddenly the challenges of finding a place to live, a job, some friends, etc. all become immeasurably easier.

It is possible to learn how to build a house on your own by trial and error, just as it is possible to establish yourself in a new city with no contacts at all. But these tasks would be formidably difficult and time-consuming, and those who undertake them with little human or social capital are prone to failure for obvious reasons.

Now that we have learned that the role of human and social capital in creating economic value and income is critical, it is startling to realize the current system of higher education does not recognize the core skills of building human and social capital as being teachable or essential to the college curriculum; students are presumed to absorb these skills (if they do at all) via osmosis or magic. This is not a modest failing; it is catastrophic for the students and the economy.

Students are recognizing that the Factory Model and the *Artificial Scarcity of Credentials* have failed to prepare them for the real economy, and employers are recognizing that student excellence in the Factory Model of Education is meaningless in terms of learning skills that are useful in their business.

According to Lazlo Bock of Google, the number of employees at the company without any higher education experience is rising:

> *What's interesting is the proportion of people without any college education at Google has increased over time as well. So we have teams where you have 14 percent of the team made up of people who've never gone to college."*

This is an admission that the current system of higher education has utterly failed to teach either the hard skills needed by employers or the soft skills students need to assemble human and social capital.

Bock's comments also suggest that those human resources managers who hire people based on their ability to meet higher education's criteria are not necessarily hiring the best candidates.

In summary, there is incontrovertible evidence that the entire higher education system is detached from the real economy: excelling in higher education has no discernible correlation to real-world skills, either for students who have learned little of applicable value or for companies which find that people who skipped the higher education system entirely may be more desirable than those who had their higher education passport stamped.

Human Capital as the Means of Production

If we think of human capital as something that is owned just like financial capital or tools, we understand why author Peter Drucker wrote that workers with human capital *own the means of production in a knowledge economy.* In other words, human capital is as essential as financial or material capital.

The *means of production* are the equipment, money and expertise needed to generate goods, services and profits. In our earlier industrial economy, these were typically factories, mines, railroads, etc., assets that require a vast amount of financial capital and human labor to operate.

In the post-industrial economy, the means of production has shifted emphasis from financial capital (money) to knowledge. As the cost of the capital tools of production—robots and digital processing—decline, the means of production are increasingly knowledge-based.

Though post-industrial economies still need capital investment, the share of labor and financial capital devoted to capital-intensive infrastructure (the electrical grid, railways, shipbuilding, etc.) declines as a percentage of total economic output (gross domestic product, GDP).

Just as the percentage of the nation's capital and labor devoted to agriculture has declined precipitously (a mere 2% of the labor force now works in agriculture), so too has the percentage of the nation's workforce and capital needed to produce steel, autos, etc.

Those parts of the economy that leverage knowledge and relatively modest capital—digital media, software, programmable robots—have expanded their share of the economy. The more productive the sector, the more profits it generates, and this attracts more capital and talent.

The cost of the tools needed to produce high-profit goods and services is declining. As a result, processes that once required massive, costly machines and large factory spaces can increasingly be done by inexpensive desktop digital fabrication tools (e.g. 3-D printers).

Information technologies (IT) that once required a large staff to operate have been automated to the point where a sole proprietor can produce output on a single inexpensive computer that until recently required a half-dozen people and multiple computers.

In other words, the means of production in the industrial age were extremely costly factories operated by thousands of low-skilled workers. The skills, talents, experience, goals and motivation of those individual workers—their human capital—had minimal impact on the overall output of the factory (with the exception of the tool-and-die workers who made the tools).

The human capital of assembly line workers was not worth much because it was interchangeable: a completely inexperienced worker could acquire the necessary skills and experience in a short time. In economic terms, the worker could not charge much of a premium for his labor because his human capital had little leverage in the production of goods, services and profits. As noted above, on an assembly line a higher-skilled worker doesn't produce much more than a lower-skilled worker. The low-skill industrial worker didn't own the means of production—his economic value was his time and ability to perform repetitive assembly tasks.

Conversely, in a knowledge-based economy, the cost of human capital dwarfs the cost of machinery and tools. A desktop digital fabrication machine might cost a few thousand dollars, and the computer that runs the design software a few hundred dollars. Training the operator costs more than the tools. This is readily apparent in local government budgets, approximately 80% of which are devoted to labor costs. Though a city owns a large capital infrastructure of roads, buildings, vehicles, etc., the cost of this physical capital is considerably less than the human capital needed to operate it.

An emerging economy is characterized by new structures of production that no longer depend on the hierarchies of large corporations and state bureaucracies, even though the value of human capital can still fluctuate with supply and demand along with every other good, service and asset. An example is the open collaboration model of assembling human capital to complete a complex project with relatively little hierarchy and management. In this model, workers opt in to complete a specified project and then move on to other work.

The financial equivalent is "crowd-funding". In a traditional economy, anyone wanting to raise money for a new enterprise had to ask for a loan from a bank or an investment from a venture-capital fund. In the crowd-funding model, funds are raised from individuals who opt in via automated software. The premium charged for the costly overhead of a bank or venture-capital fund vanishes; costs are now limited to only server space and software.

Put another way, the premiums companies can charge for financial capital and hierarchical structures of production are declining. The premiums earned by the classic advantages of corporations—access to financial capital and hierarchical management—are being eroded by new structures of finance and production.

The key point in this discussion of the means of production is this: the emerging economy is accelerating the value of human capital in both capital-intensive and labor-intensive sectors.

Economist Michael Spence has divided goods and services into two basic categories: those that can be traded globally, i.e. imported or exported, and those that cannot be traded. Work that can be outsourced to employees overseas is a tradable service—providing technical support via telephone or Internet to customers around the world, for example. Work that cannot be traded includes services that are localized, for example, repairing a porch railing.

While the infrastructure of energy, communications and transport still require massive quantities of financial and material capital, these sectors increasingly depend on high-level skills that are localized in nature and not transferable to overseas labor markets. The task of repairing an electrical line in the U.S., for example, cannot be outsourced to a worker in China or India.

Work that is programmable and that can be broken into pieces is generally tradable; work that cannot be divided into discrete tasks that can be performed remotely is not tradable. We will discuss this later in our discussion of the *matrix of work*, but the point here is that a significant amount of work cannot be programmed or performed overseas; this includes everything from lining an oil well to understanding local markets and regulations.

There is a correlation between human and social capital and the kind of work that cannot be automated or traded: these jobs break down into low-skill work (for example, janitorial work) and higher-skill labor that requires abundant human and social capital, for example maintaining an oil well's production while meeting all the regulatory requirements pertaining to the well.

As technology reduces inefficiencies and costs, the human-capital share of production grows in relative terms. As a result, financial and material capital decline as a relative percentage of the economy. For example, the number of vehicle miles driven per person in the U.S. is declining as the digital economy requires less commuting and vehicle efficiency increases.

The growing importance of human capital is best highlighted by comparing the old industrial model of production with the emerging production model. In the past, industrialists required financiers to fund the construction of huge labor-intensive factories and mines. Thousands of workers were employed in low-skill assembly jobs that only required human capital to set up the assembly process.

Now, robots have replaced assembly work and higher-value production is becoming distributed rather than centralized as tools and technology become cheaper.

When we discuss *ownership of the means of production*, many observers point to the concentration of financial capital in corporations as the controlling factor: in this view, people might own their own human capital, but they have no place to invest that capital except within the confines of large corporations. However, this assumption is becoming less applicable by the day as the tools and capital needed to produce economically valuable work decline in cost, and alternatives to centralized banking and factories sprout.

A Failing Model

As we will discuss further in Chapter 3, the trend of ever-greater centralization—of government, finance and production—has entered a terminal phase of diminishing return, as the economies of scale that powered centralization's efficiencies have led to systemic fragility and sclerosis. Centralization of finance and material capital is no longer paying systemic dividends; it has rendered our entire economy vulnerable to instability and decay.

The new emerging economy is re-establishing systemic resilience and vigor via decentralization, flexible production, transparency, and open markets—everything the currently dominant state-cartel version of capitalism is not. This is not to say that there is no role for centralized authority and production in the emerging economy; rather, the role of centralized capital and authority will play a diminishing role in the overall economy and in the creation of wealth, innovation and economic resilience.

If we accept this trend as the inevitable result of technological innovations, then we must also accept the relatively greater role for human and social capital in the emerging economy.

Cultural and Symbolic Capital

Our discussion of human and social capital would be incomplete if we did not address the implicit yet often-overlooked types of capital that have termed *cultural* and *symbolic* capital. I would add a third type of capital, *infrastructure capital*.

Returning to our earlier house-building example to help illuminate these forms of capital, let's assume the building site is far from roads, rail and river transport. The task of moving the materials and to the site has suddenly become formidable. The same can be said for generating electricity to power tools, and for delivering fuel for the generator.

Mobility, electricity and transport all depend on what we might call *infrastructure capital*, the networks available to all to move capital and goods.

Now let's imagine that the materials have been hauled at enormous expense to the site, but the infrastructure of credit does not exist: there is no way to borrow money to pay workers to build the house. We can even imagine a scenario in which the culture lacks the conceptual (symbolic) tools necessary to create a system of credit. This is the equivalent of Western Europe before the first stirrings of modern capitalism in the 13th century.

The conceptual tools of credit are an example of symbolic capital; the cultural framework that enables those conceptual tools to become commonplace is an example of cultural capital.

If we somehow manage to accumulate financial capital in an economy that does not recognize borrowing, collateral, amortization and interest (return on capital), suppose we find the building trades are controlled by a guild. Unfortunately the guild master does not trust outsiders, so there is no way to hire local labor to build the house.

As for legal recourse—there is none. Rather, the warlord/feudal lord who sold the rights to build on the parcel just lost power, and his successor revoked the rights. In this society, property rights as we understand them do not exist even as a concept, much less as an enforceable claim.

This example helps illustrate the necessary role of *infrastructure*, *cultural* and *symbolic* capital in an economy that enables the free flow of financial, material and human/social capital.

The evolution of infrastructure, cultural and conceptual/symbolic capital has not come to an end. The emerging economy is mysterious to many because it involves developing new concepts and ways of doing things. Let's consider two examples.

1. In previous eras, the mechanics of someone buying 1/100th of a mortgage on a building were cumbersome. Individuals rarely had access to the information and tools needed to assess the value of the property and the risks of the loan, and so banks performed this work for a hefty fee—the difference between the fees paid to depositors and the price the bank charged the borrower.

    This is an example of *information asymmetry*, the concept that possession of knowledge that others do not have provides a significant economic advantage. Even if individuals were able to gather the same information as banks, the mechanics of calculating and paying the monthly interest to 100 accounts was costly in time and human labor. It made practical sense to accumulate the interest in a central institution (the bank) that tallied the interest and credited depositors quarterly.

In today's digital, connected economy, there are very low cost barriers to collecting information on the building's value and the creditworthiness of the borrower, and the transactional cost of calculating and crediting the monthly interest to 100 accounts is trivial.

This example illustrates that our symbolic (i.e. conceptual) and cultural capital is evolving to enable a much more decentralized, transparent and efficient method of distributing credit, capital and risk. The value created by banks in the emerging economy is dwindling to near-zero. Indeed, in a systemic sense, the banking sector is now a parasitic, disruptive force in the economy, able to trigger global financial crises as a result of its excessive power while creating essentially nothing of value in return.

2. For our second example, let's turn to auto ownership. In the old model of private transport, in order to secure private transport, every household—and ultimately, every adult in every household—needed to buy a vehicle. This conceptual/cultural model—and the accompanying symbolism of freedom and power—created a vast industry of vehicle manufacture, fueling and maintenance.

The generation currently coming of age is significantly less attached to this model of *ownership* of private transport, as the new model of *access* to private transport is much cheaper and more flexible. However, centralized banks, manufacturers and governments still favor ownership as a model because this generates an insatiable need for credit/loans to buy the goods, a constant need to replace outdated or unfashionable models and hefty transaction/ownership taxes.

In the *access* model, full private ownership is recognized as needless and an inefficient use of capital. Why buy a car that sits unused 95% of the time? If one hundred people can share ten vehicles that are reserved digitally and priced according to demand, this enables a much lower cost for individuals and the economy at large while also creating a new digital-technology based model for generating value and profits. This model reduces the capital expended on vehicle ownership by 90%. That also means the amount of steel and energy devoted to manufacturing and maintaining vehicles declines by 90% *with no reduction in access to private transport*.

There are additional potential gains to this open-source, crowdsourced access model. It may well be that someone borrowing a car for three hours might be able to pick up and drop off another person who then shares the cost, or pick up and drop off a parcel that is making its way to its ultimate destination via a crowdsourced route using whatever means of transport are available on the most efficient route.

These two examples piggy-back efficiencies on the backbone of the open-sourced/crowd-sourced model.

These *social innovations* that leverage digital technologies are new forms of symbolic, conceptual and cultural capital. We can understand their eventual impact by comparing our current conceptual capital to that of a 12th century feudal society lacking in every form of cultural and symbolic capital that is essential to modern security and opportunity. In many ways, the current centralized post-industrial economy has more in common with a 12th century feudal society than it does with the emerging economy.

Centralization and the 100%private ownership model are the modern-day equivalents of a limited, static, impoverished 12th century feudal economy, and the current system of higher education, along with its financial foundation, the *artificial scarcity of credentials*, are key cogs in this limiting, impoverishing and parasitic neo-feudal system.

Mastery as the Means of Production

Familiarity with a field is rarely enough to create much economic value. Familiarity may be enough for low-skill commodity labor, but the purpose of higher education is to prepare students to acquire skills that create significant economic value.

This is why the goal of all learning aimed at creating economic value is *mastery of a practice or skillset* - for only mastery generates a premium.

In the context of the previous section, we can define mastery in an economic sense as *owning the means of production in a knowledge economy* (for mastery is a key component of human capital). All the other components of human capital—self-discipline, learning how to learn, etc.—serve the goal of attaining economically valuable mastery.

Consider the case of an experienced handyperson who can troubleshoot and repair dozens of different problems in dwellings. The hand tools needed to perform the vast majority of these repair/maintenance tasks are mass-produced and relatively inexpensive. The financial and physical capital needed to create value as a handyperson is modest; the largest capital expense is transport to various jobs.

By themselves, these tools cannot possibly create any economic value or premium; they are useless. In the hands of an inexperienced, low-skill worker, they will more likely be a force of value destruction rather than value creation. *Only in the hands of an experienced, high-skill knowledge worker can the tools create value.*

The somewhat-knowledgeable handyperson will lack the experience and skills to quickly and correctly assess the problem and determine the lowest-cost, most efficient means to repair the problem. The less motivated, less skilled worker may well take ten times as long to make the repair as the worker who has mastered all the required trades, and may well select repair options that cost more and are less effective.

In other words, mastery—deep expertise based on experience and *ownership of the work*—is the key element to value creation. Mastery is what creates a premium for human capital.

Mastery is not just a mix of knowledge, expertise and experience: it also requires *ownership of the work*, meaning that the master performs all work as if he owns every aspect of it: the process, the final product and the reputation that arises from the results of the work.

The worker who does not own their work is careless and slipshod, an attitude expressed in phrases such as "I only work here," "close enough for government work," and "there's no point it doing it right, nobody else does." The worker who owns knowledge and expertise but is incapable of owning their work can never achieve mastery.

It is vital that we understand that mastery is not just a collection of hard skills; it is also a value system of ownership of all work, no matter how menial or trivial it may appear to the outsider. In a very real sense, the worker who doesn't own his work does not really own the means of production, no matter how skilled or experienced he may be.

To illustrate the mindset of mastery, let's consider garden maintenance as an example. The master gardener treats each of the yards in his care as if he owned it, and as if every aspect of his care is a reflection of his reputation and skill. It doesn't matter if the garden's owner is rich or poor or pleasant or unpleasant; the work is done equally well for all because the master gardener 'owns' it all.

To establish and maintain a livelihood in the emerging economy, students must be able to constantly build economically valuable mastery in their chosen field. Simply acquiring generalized knowledge will not be enough to create value.

In traditional economies, mastery is gained by serving a long unpaid apprenticeship with a master craftsperson. The master often owns his/her own workshop, and provides the apprentices with room and board. In exchange for years of hard labor, the master teaches the apprentices the processes and skills of the craft. Such apprentice-master craftsperson arrangements still exist in the traditional handcrafts of Japan.

American labor law requires payment for labor (other than the loophole for unpaid internships), thus long paid apprenticeships are impractical for most small enterprises. The Nearly Free University model offers another model of achieving mastery that makes judicious use of mentors/masters in workshop/lab settings. We will discuss this model after we understand the matrix of work.

Economically Valuable Skills and the Matrix of Work

All knowledge is not equal. Knowledge overall may have value, but only certain kinds of knowledge lead to skills that have economic value in the real world. In a dynamic economy (and dynamism is a key feature of the emerging economy), the economic value of specific skills may change rapidly for a number of fundamental reasons: the supply and demand for labor/skills may change, technology may radically reduce the need for a wide swath of human labor, and geopolitical, environmental or financial crises may transform the foundations of entire industries. Since knowledge and instruction are both essentially free now, the focus of higher education should be on skills that create economic value.

What categories of work will be economically valuable in the emerging economy? While there are many ways to slice-and-dice work, the most insightful way is to differentiate between three basic types:

1. Work that can be commoditized, i.e. work that can be automated or performed by machines. If the state of completion and the procedures and processes needed to reach that completion can be specified, then some or all of the task/work may be programmable and thus able to be automated.

2. Work in which the state of completion and the processes used to create value cannot be specified. This includes creative, synthesizing work as well as some types of managerial and tradecraft work.

   As a general rule, low-skill work is more easily specified and thus automated, while high-skill work is less easily specified and therefore more difficult to commoditize/replace with machines. This does not mean higher-skill work cannot be automated; as we shall see, high-skill work that is based on process can often be automated.

   Work that is difficult to specify generally requires a range of mastery (i.e. experiential knowledge and skills) that can be flexibly applied in the analog (real) world. Yard maintenance offers an example: an automated lawnmower could be programmed to mow an expansive lawn to near-perfection, but the cost of programming a machine to care for dozens of different types of flowering plants, trees, shrubs, etc., semi-randomly sited in a complex garden without clear pathways would be prohibitive given the comparatively low cost and high flexibility of human labor.

3. Work whose economic value is derived from human (i.e. non-programmable) connections of empathy, touch, emotional support, etc. This is called *high touch* work. Examples include medical care,

mentoring, sales and psychotherapy. Interactions in which human connections constitute much of the economic value are at the high end of the *high touch/low touch* continuum. An example of low touch is shopping online, where the processes and interactions are automated.

Some types of high touch work are relatively low-skill; others require high levels of knowledge and experience. The matrix created by these sliding scales helps us identify work that can be automated and what kinds of work will still require human labor and expertise.

1. Low-skill / high-skill

2. Low-touch / high-touch

3. Work than can be specified to completion / work that cannot be specified to completion

There are two other factors that influence the economic value of skills:

4. The sensitivity of output to skills and mastery

5. How much of the skill is process-based

I am indebted to writer Michael O. Church for his explanation of the difference between types of work that he characterizes as *convex* and *concave*, a terminology derived from charting the input/output curve of skills/knowledge to productive work. One type of work is relatively insensitive to higher skills and knowledge, while the other is sensitive to high levels of skill and experience, i.e. mastery.

Another term for *concave work* is *commodity work*, i.e. work that can be programmed or performed by machines. This is work where the qualitative and quantitative difference between beginners and experienced workers is significant and the difference between low-skill and high-skill workers is relatively insignificant.

In our yard maintenance example, a low-skill but experienced worker is significantly more productive at mowing the lawn than the beginner. But a master gardener with high levels of knowledge and experience isn't much faster at mowing the lawn than the low-skill worker.

In *convex work*, the difference in productivity between the beginner and the worker with some experience is insignificant but the difference between middling experience and mastery is large. Writing software is often used as an example of convex work, as the learning curve is steep enough that workers with some experience are not much more productive than beginners, while the highly experienced (and thus highly skilled) workers are an order of magnitude more productive than workers with some experience and skills.

In fields that depend heavily on creativity or innovation, the economic value of the work done by the most experienced, high-skill people is many times higher than that of middling-skill, less experienced workers.

The other factor is the nature of the skill: is it a process-based skill that is repeatable in a routine fashion, or is it a diagnostic, *experiential-sensitive* skill?

Some skills can be gained relatively quickly while others require a long apprenticeship. While we tend to associate long, steep learning curves with fields such as medicine and law that are widely assumed to be impervious to automation, some aspects of these specialized fields are being automated, for example, primary screening in electrocardiography or radiography. In other words, though we assume skills that are difficult to master cannot be performed by machines, this overlooks the critical distinction between specialized knowledge that is *process-based* (i.e. is only needed once to set up the process) versus work that requires the flexible application of experience that cannot be entirely reduced to a set routine.

A process must have a specifiable input, output and set of standards and procedures.

Locating tumors on x-rays, for example, is a high-skill task that is largely specifiable and can be performed by a machine. Unlike a human, the machine doesn't get tired and is thus less likely to make errors in the screening process.

The preparation of many legal documents is also process-based: once the template is set so that it complies with applicable codes and laws, a low-skill worker or customer can provide the input.

Many professions have digitized their process-based expertise into computer programs that are not available to the general public; the cost of operating the program is low, but the price is high because the product must be validated by the preparer. Examples include income tax returns, real estate appraisals and legal documents such as incorporation papers.

In other words, the work has already been automated but the high cost to the customer does not reflect this, as the validation by the preparer establishes a false scarcity value. For example, real estate appraisal software generates appraisals for a very low cost, but the validation by the licensed appraiser creates a scarcity value because the number of licensed appraisers is limited. This is the same mechanism the higher education cartel uses to enforce an artificially high cost for college diplomas.

On the other end of the *process-based* scale, learning to treat patients with a friendly, caring manner while performing low-skilled labor is relatively easy to learn, but this high-touch value cannot be offered by a machine. A robot may be able to perform the physical work of serving the patient but the human touch that lends comfort cannot be replaced – although some studies have found that people respond positively to robots that mimic human signifiers of caring, so it may be that in some cases, robots with higher-touch capabilities will begin to replace high-touch human workers. Whether we approve of this or not is beside the point; if the quality of care increases and costs decrease, this trend will accelerate. Alternatively, both robot and human care may be offered, and customers will be asked to pay more for human service.

The *process-based /experiential-sensitive* continuum of work is not necessarily either/or. For example, welding is a difficult and time-consuming skill to master. In process-based work such as standardized parts moving down an assembly line, a robot welder is much faster and more accurate than a human welder. In customized, one-off work, however, the human welder and the welding robot become a complementary team; the robot handles the welding that it is optimized to do, and the human does the welding that it is impractical for the robot perform.

The human welder is qualified not only to program the welding robot, but to do work that is too small in scope (for example, field repairs) to justify delivering and programming a robot. A welder's skill is both process-based and experiential-dependent. This is true of many professions, including law, medicine and engineering.

Work in which the input and output criteria, standards and procedural steps lend themselves easily and readily to being digitized will be automated; that trend will continue. As the cost of digital processing declines, automation becomes increasingly cost-effective. As the ability of digital technology to perform work faster, better and cheaper than human labor advances, more types of work become commoditized.

This includes relatively low-skilled, low-wage work in fields such as agriculture and fast food preparation and higher-skill white-collar tasks that can be programmed. As the wages and benefits paid to human workers increase, the cost advantages of replacing human labor with software also rises.

The unifying characteristics of work that is difficult to automate are *mastery of skills that cannot be specified as routine processes, flexibility and high touch*. These skills—along with the eight essential skills—are key characteristics of human and social capital.

Once we understand these dynamics of creating economic value, we can design an approach to higher education that gives students the tools needed to establish and maintain a livelihood. First and foremost, this requires *self-learning to mastery* in skills that are not readily automated and the eight essential skills listed in Chapter 1.

If there is one prediction we can make with confidence, it is that the nature and value of work will be constantly changing. To make the most of our understanding of work, we need to explore the concept of *premium*, i.e. how work creates value.

The Premium of Labor

Let's start with the three fundamental components of the economy:

1. the open market (free enterprise),

2. the state (government), and

3. the community, i.e. all the activity and assets that are not priced by the market or controlled by the state. Examples include churches, neighborhood groups and non-profit organizations. These interact

with both the market and state, but the purpose of the organization is not to reap a profit or enforce regulations and laws.

In the open market economy, revenues must exceed expenses, i.e. the enterprise must generate a profit. Costs include

- materials,
- labor and overhead (labor overhead includes employer's tax payments, unemployment insurance, etc., while general overhead includes office rent, accounting, etc.),
- capital investment (replacing or upgrading equipment and software), and

If the enterprise loses money, it will eventually close, or bankrupt whatever entity is subsidizing the losses. As author Peter Drucker noted, enterprises do not have profits, they only have expenses. If the costs of producing the good or service exceed the market value of the product, then cost must be reduced or the enterprise will lose money and shut down.

The current global economy is characterized by over-capacity: the supply of goods and services is larger than the demand. There are too many steel mills, hotel rooms, factories making TVs, etc., and relatively few manufactured goods that are scarce. This forces enterprises to reduce their input costs—the costs of production—to reap a profit.

In many cases, labor is the most expensive component of production costs. Labor must generate a premium, a gain in value beyond the cost of the labor. For example, if a company pays an employee $40,000 a year in wages, the firm must also pay labor overhead and benefits, costs which may add 50% to the base wage. The company must also generate a gross profit large enough to fund capital investment and general overhead. Lastly, there is no point in hiring the worker if the worker's labor doesn't add value, i.e. a return on the capital invested in the enterprise.

Thus a worker paid $40,000 must generate at least $100,000 of additional economic value to justify his employment. If labor cannot generate enough surplus value to pay for capital investment, general overhead and a return on capital, the enterprise will suffer steady losses.

Since a robot and its digital software do not need healthcare, unemployment and disability insurance or a pension plan, the robot costs 50% less than the human worker even if the robot's operational costs equal the base wage paid to the human worker.

As the costs of digital technology fall and the ability of this technology to replace human labor increases, the premium generated by labor declines: if a robot that costs $20,000 a year to operate can replace a human worker being paid $40,000, the value of the human labor just fell to the robot's operational cost, i.e. $20,000 per year. *Labor that cannot be replaced by software/machines generates a premium, especially if the labor is in a sector where prices are high due to scarcity of the good or service being produced.*

This explains why cartels are able to pay high wages for labor: by creating an artificial scarcity, the cartel can charge high prices.

Outside of cartels, the market dictates the scarcity or abundance of supply and demand for goods, services and labor. When there is an oversupply of goods, services and labor, the price of all three falls.

As technology replaces human labor, people naturally seek work in whatever sectors are less impacted by technology. These tend to be cartels and the state, which are immune to price discovery and competition by virtue of monopoly (the state) or artificial scarcity (cartels). As the number of jobs that cannot be replaced by technology declines, the supply of labor increases. This supply and demand imbalance tends to drive wages down, as more workers compete for increasingly scarce jobs.

The state pays high wages by taxing the productive workers and enterprises in the private sector. This gives states the power to pay above-market rates to labor, in effect subsidizing the state's labor force. A subsidy is not a premium. In other words, if the state pays above-market wages, it doesn't mean the state labor is creating a premium; it simply means the taxpayers are subsidizing the state workers' higher pay. This is not a value judgment; it is simply a statement of economics.

Let's take state-mandated labor at gasoline stations as an example. Some states require that gasoline must be pumped by paid staff. This is a policy decision that creates jobs that would not exist if customers pumped their own gasoline. The jobs are subsidized by buyers of gasoline (and perhaps taxpayers; the details vary from state to state).

There is a premium generated by someone pumping gasoline for you, but the premium is only as large as what customers willingly pay extra for the service. The state forces customers to subsidize these jobs as a policy decision; it is not a market-based assessment of the value of gasoline-pumping.

If having gasoline pumped for you costs 10% more in the open market, then that is the premium labor creates for that service. Any sum beyond that is a subsidy.

Ultimately, all state spending and subsidies are paid by the surplus generated by non-state workers and enterprises. That means there is a limit on how much the state can subsidize labor. The Federal government could print unlimited sums of money, but eventually this will destroy the economy. (For more on this, please see my book *Why Things Are Falling Apart and What We Can Do About It*.)

Outside the state and cartels (which are generally enforced by the state), labor can charge a premium if it is scarce (i.e. few people have the necessary skills) and it creates high value in the marketplace. As noted earlier, *mastery of skills that cannot be fully specified as routine processes, flexibility and high touch* create economic value.

Conversely, if the skills are not scarce and/or the value created is low, the wages will also be low. This is why fast-food preparation is paid relatively modest wages. The work is hard and fast-paced but doesn't require high skills, so the surplus value is relatively low. How much premium are people willing to pay to be served fast food by a human worker? We can ask the same question of retail purchases. Many people like being served by a human, and will pay a premium for this service. Others would prefer to order online or be served by a machine if the cost is lower.

Being served fast food is low touch; there is little value in the human interaction. Buying fashionable clothing is for many a high touch experience, and people are often willing to pay a premium to be served by a knowledgeable staff person. In general, people won't pay premiums for low touch interactions, and so these processes are prone to being automated.

Since one fast-food meal is relatively similar to other fast-food meals, there is little premium placed on the skill of the preparer. Low touch, low skill work has little premium, so the benefits of automation are compelling to employers facing ever-higher labor overhead costs in an economy burdened with over-capacity.

In contrast, a restaurant can offer a high-touch, high-skill experience and thus it can charge a premium for its ambience, serve staff and freshly prepared meals. The labor generates the premium: a restaurant with an abundance of ambience will soon be deserted if the staff is incompetent and the food poorly prepared.

Some labor generates its value less from specialized skills and more from high touch. These workers do not need lengthy skills-based training to create value; the value is created by high touch characteristics such as empathy and the generalized professionalism embodied by the eight essential skills.

As we have seen, there are five sliding scales of value creation. The higher the worker's level on each scale, the larger the premium his/her labor can generate:

1. low-skill / high-skill
2. low-touch / high-touch
3. Work that cannot be specified to completion
4. The sensitivity of output to skills and mastery
5. How much of the skill is process-based

The purpose and goal of the Nearly Free University is to open a pathway for everyone to master the eight essential skills of building human and social capital, and thereby gain the means to acquire whatever specialized skills they desire to own.

Contrast this with the current system of higher education, which does not recognize the skills needed to build human and social capital as the core curriculum. The current system has little connection to work or the ways labor generates economic value and premium. No wonder this high-priced cartel has failed to prepare students for employment in the emerging economy.

What Can Be Self-Taught and What Must Be Learned from Others?

Work in the emerging economy will be dynamic, and most work will require a lifetime of learning to generate higher premiums/wages. Much of this will be self-learning, where the student is also the teacher. At certain stages in the process, the guidance of a master/mentor in a workshop/lab environment greatly leverages learning.

What can be self-taught and what must be learned from others? The first short answer is virtually everything can be learned—i.e. self-taught—and so the one essential skill is learning how to learn in a structured manner that leads to economically valuable mastery.

Beyond learning how to learn, the question boils down to: *at which critical junctures of the learning process is mentoring most effective?* As someone who has learned a number of different skills both on my own and via on-the-job tutelage of mentor/masters, I am sensitive to key points in the learning curve where a master/mentor can help the student advance more quickly. I have also found that virtually all economically valuable learning is learned by doing. *Do the thing and you shall have the power*, advised Ralph Waldo Emerson, for there is no substitute for engaging in real work and being responsible for the output.

The second short answer is that *the eight critical skills must be practiced in real-world settings to be effectively mastered.* As noted in Chapter 1, conventional lectures and MOOCs can help students learn subject matter, but *learning skills requires doing.* We all understand this is true in the practical skills of cooking, carpentry, driving a vehicle, playing a musical instrument, etc. No amount of passively watching a lecture, either live or online, will teach a student how to cook, drive an auto, play guitar, build a cabinet or operate a digital fabrication device. The current system recognizes this in training students for traditional tradecraft jobs in two-year community college programs, but it is equally applicable for white-collar work.

This also holds true for the eight critical skills: no amount of passively watching lectures can possibly teach students to collaborate effectively and professionally with others and approach life and work with an entrepreneurial toolbox of skills.

We can separate learning into three basic types:

1. Passive learning in the factory model, where student attend lectures or view MOOCs and follow the same curriculum as thousands or even millions of other students.

2. Learning by doing, i.e. performing economically valuable work on one's own or in a job setting.

3. Learning the finer points of skills under the guidance of a master/mentor in a workshop/lab.

It is certainly possible to achieve mastery on one's own; this is the only path open to those carving out new pathways of knowledge. But as Isaac Newton observed, "If I have seen further it is by standing on the shoulders of giants."

This is the structural value of the workshop or laboratory: the student must do the work on their own, with the master/mentor assessing their progress and offering guidance at intervals. If the curriculum is well-designed, a handful of workshops per semester will suffice.

The master/mentor is not the only source of help. Other students at the same or more advanced levels can also provide peer-to-peer tutoring and mentoring; this is a structural feature of the workshop/lab setting.

We can now discern the outlines of the Nearly Free University's curriculum and cost structure: the high-cost presence of a master/mentor is only effective at key points of leverage. The rest of the time, the students can learn general knowledge on their own, along with applied knowledge by doing the actual work in a workshop/lab setting where peer-to-peer/teaching assistant collaboration is the norm.

In other words, general knowledge can be learned on one's own within the essentially free universe of massively open online courses (MOOCs) and other online media. In essence, this universe has digitized and commoditized the Factory Model of broadcast lectures and mass-produced textbooks, workbooks and tests. Conversely, the core curriculum of the eight essential skills must be learned by *doing* in a workshop/lab environment, where collaboration, criticism, professionalism, etc., are practiced in a simulation of the workplace.

Ultimately, the goal of higher education boils down to helping students gain the eight essential skills and learn how to reach to a level of economically useful mastery on their own.

Achieving mastery is quite a different process than scoring good grades within the Factory Model of higher education. Mastery is not about learning material; it is about ownership. Mastery cannot be taught, it can only be gained by experience, which means practicing on one's own, and accepting disappointment, failure, criticism and guidance.

Like all learning, it requires perseverance, i.e. self-motivation, and self-discipline, skills which are presumed to be taught in primary and secondary education. Given its key role in self-learning and mastery, however, the Nearly Free University curriculum must encourage the development of self-motivation.

Developing and Maintaining Motivation

One key component of self-learning is maintaining self-motivation and self-discipline.

The implicit assumption of conventional pedagogy is that students must be constantly motivated by teachers to learn. This may reflect the inherent weaknesses of the Factory Model of Education rather than human nature, as our minds are hard-wired to continuously refine our knowledge and skillsets.

The Factory Model doesn't lend itself to sustaining motivation; indeed, the physical factory model pioneered by Henry Ford in the early 20th century was unpopular with workers, many of whom quit after a few days. The only motivator that improved the abysmal worker-retention rate was significantly increasing the pay to overcome the workers' natural resistance to mind-numbingly boring hard labor.

We should not be surprised that the Factory Model of Education has failed for many of the same reasons.

An implicit assumption in higher education is that students already possess self-motivation and self-discipline, and so the curriculum need not take motivation into account.

Studies of adults pursuing difficult long-term goals such as weight loss find the god-like powers of self-discipline and motivation assumed by higher education are not widespread, even within the cohort who graduated from college. Rather, these studies find peer support is the one predictive factor in maintaining weight loss.

Assuming that students watching MOOC courses alone at home can learn the eight essential skills and master applying these skills is a fatally flawed assumption. Nurturing self-motivation and peer support will be a key success factor in the Nearly Free University curriculum.

To nurture motivation, we first must understand its sources. There are a number of built-in sources of motivation: our natural curiosity, for example, leads to learning. Learning practical skills is also inherently empowering, as acquiring new skills boosts our position in the social and economic hierarchy. This drive for self-betterment is a key source of motivation and self-discipline.

What motivates people to become their own teacher, i.e. to self-learn? As a general rule, their motivation springs from a desire to learn how to do a specific task. This desire may arise from curiosity or from the desire to improve earnings or social standing or change some important aspect of your life; motivation may have a number of origins. In terms of systematically teaching someone how to learn on their own, the one essential the student must grasp is that the ultimate goal of the self-learner is *mastery of a practice or skillset*.

The most compelling motivation is to learn how to do something well enough that the student acquires the personal satisfaction and economic power of mastery.

Acquiring Mastery

Do the thing and you shall have the power, advised Ralph Waldo Emerson, and this is what we observe in self-learners: they are itching to do the thing and gain the powers of applied knowledge and practical skills.

Learning is not a smooth curve; it is inherently bumpy, and certain phases of the learning process are so difficult that even motivated students may become discouraged. These are the critical points where outside resources can apply leverage.

There are two basic structures that help the self-learning student over these rough spots:

1.   peers pursuing the same goal, and

2.   the mentor-apprentice relationship.

The first critical point is in the initial learning curve. Beginners may be discouraged by their lack of initial progress, which is why instruction that teaches by *doing* rather than *reading* rewards their desire to start doing the thing they're interested in learning. Once they've received the encouragement provided by successfully taking the first step, they are better prepared to endure a steep learning curve in which rewards may be few and far between.

Consider teaching a young child how to ride a bike. If you lecture them about the techniques of riding, the various parts of the bicycle, the traffic rules governing riding on streets, etc. —the generalized knowledge that characterizes the factory model—they soon become distracted, bored or frustrated.

Or you can lead them straight to their bike and teach them to ride it. My technique for teaching someone how to ride a bike is very simple: after making sure the child is properly positioned on the bike, I hold one handle bar and the seat and start guiding the bike forward. After they experience what it feels like to be moving forward in a stable fashion, pedaling, steering, and braking while the bike is under my control, I announce that I'm going to take my hands off the bike for a second or two. In those few seconds before I resume control of their bike, they are riding the bike on their own.

The momentum alone keeps the bike moving forward, and their initial wobble is to be expected. But since I take control of the bike almost immediately, very little can go awry. The next time, I let them ride freely for a few more seconds. As the time they are under their own power lengthens to 10 seconds and then 20 seconds, they have essentially learned how to ride a bike. In a few minutes of *accretive, structured steps*, they have gained the rudimentary skill and experience needed to build confidence.

Some skills are inherently difficult and therefore arduous to learn, for example, learning to play guitar. The initial learning curve is very steep, as the raw beginner will have difficulty even holding down the strings cleanly enough to generate a clear note.

In the factory model, the student would start by memorizing the fretboard and learning basic music theory and chords. Motivation drags under this diet of passive instruction. The *do the thing and you shall have the power* method might be to have the student list a few of his favorite songs, and then locate the song sheets/chord progressions on the Internet. The instructor would select the easiest song to play and start by impressing upon the student the need to work very diligently every day for a full week to learn the song. The student would be shown the necessary chords—accretive, structured steps that lead to experiencing the power of new skills—and told that the only way to master the chords is with repeated practice, even when the results of the effort appear minimal.

Once the student successfully learns one song of his choice, no matter how coarse the playing might be, the student will have learned enough to experience the exhilaration of newly acquired real-world skills.

The second key leverage point is to guide the student to the *experience of mastery*. The advance to an experience of mastery—in our example, playing these few chords again and again until the progression is clean, smooth and natural—requires self-discipline, time management and a number of other aspects of the eight essential skills. It is at this critical point of leverage that self-discipline and the structure of the learning process become the paramount lessons: without self-discipline and structure, learning is piecemeal and cannot develop the ultimate skill of *learning to mastery*.

In the Asian tradition, the neophyte apprentice spends the first few years of apprenticeship doing low-skill, repetitive tasks to learn both self-discipline and the basics of the tradecraft. The objective is threefold:

1. To impress upon the student that the knowledge and skills being passed down to him are highly valued and cannot be gained easily;

2. To guide the student to the experience of mastery in the most basic skills of the trade; and

3. To instill self-discipline and the ability to persevere despite the rewards (empowerment, higher social standing, money) being slim to non-existent.

In other words, the objective is to teach the student that mastery of the trade can only be gained by rigorously following a structured series of accretive steps. Though it is tempting to think one can leapfrog from a few hastily-learned basics to near-mastery, this is the path to failure: each step in the trade must be mastered before it is possible to advance to the next. The master imposes this discipline not as punishment but as the necessarily rigorous path to mastery.

The authority of the mentor-master is not enforced by the government or an institution; rather, the authority flows solely from the mastery and the willingness to teach apprentices. These two traits are the source of the respect given to masters by their peers and apprentices.

This philosophy and program of learning is also the foundation of all martial arts instruction: there can be no mastery without rigorous adherence to strict rules of conduct and incessant practice of a highly structured series of accretive steps--deliberate, dedicated time spent focusing on improving one's skills. This is the core of gaining mastery, and the ability to self-learn to mastery is the core skill needed to establish and earn a livelihood in the emerging economy.

Once the student has experienced learning as a process of *accretive, structured steps* that when pursued with self-discipline leads to the *experience of mastery,* he or she has gained the foundational skills of self-learning and the self-confidence to apply them to new fields.

The third point of leverage is the actual application of newly acquired skills to real-world tasks and settings. The Nearly Free University model recognizes that few students or mentors have sufficient time or money to spend years working together without compensation. The NFU model recognizes the indispensable role of the mentor/master in the workshop/lab setting, but it seeks to leverage the key points in the learning process where the mentor/master has the biggest influence.

The Student as Teacher

Learning on one's own is often referred to as self-taught, but perhaps the more accurate description is *the student is also the teacher*. This term covers self-learning and students teaching each other. Peer-to-peer collaborative learning can occur in a workshop, lab, dingy basement or under a tree; it is not tethered to the factory model of pedagogy (i.e. broadcast lecture, solitary study and regurgitation of material on a test) nor to the administrative structure of a college.

What is necessary is a structured course of study and a structure that enables and encourages collaboration, what we might term an *ecosystem of collaboration*.

Sustainable careers in the emerging economy are increasingly an interconnected *ecosystem of collaboration* rather than a conventionally defined job within a hierarchy. Even within conventional careers, traditional areas of knowledge are spilling over and overlapping with previously distinct fields of expertise, requiring new levels of collaboration.

In other words, the Nearly Free University model of student collaboration within structured labs/workshops mirrors the emerging economy's ecosystem of collaboration.

There are a number of different aspects to *the student is also the teacher*.

1. The Nearly Free University model of structured workshops/labs, *adaptive learning* and an ecosystem of collaboration teaches students to structure learning and collaborate on their own.

2. Collaboration occurs in two overlapping ecosystems: in person and globally "face to face" online. While we often collaborate with the

same people in both areas, the two systems are not interchangeable and require slightly different skills and structures.

3. Peer-to-peer collaboration and teaching is now possible via digital media, though this augments rather than replaces collaboration in real-world settings.

4. Technology has broadened the opportunities for the student to become the teacher via software-enabled adaptive learning. Anecdotally, developing-world students given appropriately programmed tablet computers (basic models now cost about $45) can learn subjects on their own by playing preprogrammed educational games without any teacher at all.

   In other words, in areas where teachers are unaffordable or scarce, cheap tablet computers and well-devised games and exercises provide learning for the cost of recharging the batteries.

   One of the key weaknesses in the Factory Model is the *one size fits all* nature of the curriculum and method of teaching. The rigidity of this *one size fits all* model is supposedly offset by the flexibility of the teacher, but in practice no teacher can possibly prepare 30 different curricula and customize methods of teaching for 30 students.

5. Since the cost of reproducing and distributing digital lessons is essentially zero, an ever-widening spectrum of instructional videos offers each student a range of teaching approaches and methods which traverse the same material by different pathways. Outside the boundaries of the MOOC model, shorter, targeted instructional videos are available at *YouTube University*, my term for the universe of high-level instruction available on YouTube. These lessons guide students through specific steps of complex processes. Individual students can review and then select the curriculum, teacher and approach within the MOOC and YouTube University spheres that is "best of class" for their learning style and aptitudes. Software can guide this process in what is known as adaptive learning: shaping the pace and the curriculum to the personality, interests and learning preferences of each individual.

In this model, the primary task of teaching (formally known as pedagogy) is organizing the multitude of instructional options into a coherent menu of choices that aligns with the curriculum. The task of guiding students to the most appropriate instructions can be automated and augmented by mentors familiar with the curriculum choices and peer recommendations.

Instruction in this model becomes an open, transparent and nearly free marketplace in which students select "best of class" for their individual needs. As in all such transparent markets, a handful of instructors and programs will likely capture most of the student mindshare, but a wealth of competing programs will be available to fit students' individual preferences.

It would be difficult to tell at a glance whether students taking an online lesson are doing so on their own or as part of a NFU curriculum. The difference is the NFU coursework is a structured curriculum that includes a workshop or lab component with both real-world and online ecosystems of collaboration.

The Nearly Free University Template

We have reached point where we can assemble the ideas presented in this chapter into a curriculum template for the Nearly Free University.

Our critique of the current higher education system had four components:

1. Financially it is a cartel that extracts high premiums from an artificial scarcity of credentials.

2. The system is disconnected from the real world of work in the emerging economy.

3. The system's curriculum and methodology is the obsolete Factory Model of Education.

4. The system conflates scholarship and research with teaching, subsidizing the top-heavy costs of bureaucracy, scholarship and research with student fees.

In contrast, the Nearly Free University model is based on a three-part solution:

1. Accredit the student, not the school.

2. Structure learning such that it no longer depends on large physical campuses and costly administration.

3. Tailor the curriculum to the needs of the real-world emerging economy and the methods of learning to the individual student.

Attributes of the NFU Template

1. The curriculum would be designed by working professionals in each field to align with the real-world needs of enterprises and employers.

2. The curriculum, pacing and style of learning are aligned to the personality, aptitudes, interests and preferences of each individual student. This adaptive learning is guided by continuous feedback on the students' progress. Automated software enables low-cost delivery of this model.

3. Online courses would not be scheduled in arbitrary semesters; they would be offered year-round. Since the student is accredited rather than the institution, there is nothing sacred about the four-year time period for an undergraduate degree or two years for a graduate or law degree. If one student completes the requisite exams and projects in a year, and another student takes five years, the process of earning accreditation remains the same.

4. All the general education coursework can be done online with freely available texts and material. Local students taking the same course may gather for peer-to-peer tutoring and learning, but these assemblies are self-organizing and free of administration and cost. This would include science, technology, engineering and math (STEM) coursework from organizations such as Saylor.org.

5. The eight essential skills require collaboration in workshops or laboratories, under the guidance of a working professional master/mentor rather than a scholar. The workshop/lab requires actual production of economic value in a workplace setting. Ideally, the workshops/labs occur in actual workplaces.

6. Accreditation for each subject is designed by working professionals in each field, in a form appropriate for the subject. A technical

subject may require a proctored examination, modeled on the state bar exam for attorneys or the licensing test for architects. In other subjects, accreditation may require completion of a project overseen by the equivalent of a flight instructor, i.e. a master who stakes his/her own reputation on the student's accreditation.

7. Research and scholarship must be funded by sources other than students.

8. The working professional master/mentor is paid a modest fee for part-time supervision of the workshop or lab; the motivation is not high pay or a secure career, but sharing working knowledge with students.

9. The cost of all digitally distributed general education and accreditation exams is near-zero. The cost of workshops is measured in hundreds of dollars (2013 dollars) rather than thousands of dollars (see below for an example). The cost of accreditation is kept near-zero by opening the field to non-profit organizations.

10. The enrollment and accreditation process is transparent and automated.

11. The NFU is open to all regardless of age, ethnicity, class, gender, faith or nationality.

12. Learning is untethered from the campus, administrative costs, and the student loan machine.

The NFU Workshop/Lab Model

In terms of *social capital*—the ability to work productively and professionally with others and to share ideas, techniques, processes and critiques—collaboration in the workshop or lab is the essential foundry of effective learning. In terms of *human capital* and *mastery*, the workshop/lab is the foundation of experiential learning—the kind that assembles effective skills and generates economic value.

Now that desktop digital fabrication and other lab equipment can be bought for a few thousand dollars (or in some cases assembled for a few hundred dollars), the justification for constructing hugely expensive buildings on sprawling campuses vanishes. It's worth recalling that groundbreaking theater groups such as Monty Python found their comedic footing in dingy basements devoid of state-of-the-art equipment. The many collaborative workshops that don't require lab or foundry equipment might just as well be held under a tree in good weather, or in a café, or in an enterprise willing to host an occasional workshop, rather than in a formal classroom on a campus.

The NFU model prefers workshops and labs be held in workplaces for several reasons, including:

1. There is no substitute for on-the-job learning in a real workplace.

2. The costs of the workplace have already been paid by the enterprise, and so letting students use a bit of space for a few hours essentially costs the business nothing. There is no reason to hold a workshop or lab in a business that charges more than a modest fee for use of the space.

Adult education programs offer a variety of cost templates for NFU workshops and labs. The first requirement is that masters/mentors lead workshops/labs not necessarily as a source of their primary income but as a part-time endeavor to share their working knowledge and reap the rewards of mentoring students.

For example, let's suppose that a digital fabrication lab of ten students guided by one mentor covers a particular subject in depth in ten workshops, roughly the equivalent of a weekly lab in a conventional quarter. The mentor is paid $30 an hour as an independent contractor or $900 for ten three-hour workshops, while the lab sponsors that let the students use their equipment charge $30 per session or $300 for the ten workshops. Each student is thus responsible for $120 in direct fees, and perhaps $30 for the administrative server costs and the course exam or project testing for a total cost of $150 per student.

Since the current higher education system sees fit to issue an undergraduate diploma for 30 credits (i.e. ten classes) of coursework in a specific subject (i.e. the major), then ten workshops would suffice for accreditation in a major subject and, more importantly, experience in the eight essential skills and mastery of a subject. The total cost of ten workshops (not counting materials consumed in the lab) is 10 X $150 or

$1,500, while the cost of thirty general education online courses is $30 X 30 or $900.

Thus the total cost of thirty general education classes and ten mentor-supervised workshops would be $2,400. If you think adding 50% is necessary to these costs, the total cost rises to $3,600. Since many households pay in excess of $100 per month for smartphone telecom plans, taking thirty classes and ten workshops in three years (summers need not be taken off) would cost no more than what tens of millions of people pay for phone plans.

In terms of scholarships, $3,600 for forty courses is within reach of community churches, service clubs, extended families, local enterprises and myriad other funding sources.

The foundation of classical capitalism is transparent competition. If a university wants to offer its existing classrooms and labs for Nearly Free University classes and workshops, they are free to do so providing the fees they charge ($150 per workshop and $30 per online class) are competitive.

Those within the cartel might claim that scholars and professors make the best mentors. The NFU model neither refutes nor confirms that claim; it opens the role of workshop/lab mentor to everyone with experiential mastery and a desire to help students acquire mastery. The spectrum of potential mentors is greatly expanded, to the ultimate benefit of students and society.

Those mentors who are effective teachers will gain the accreditation of students and those who hire them; those are the only meaningful forms of mentor-master accreditation. Academic standing within the cartel loses its meaning once students are accredited directly.

Many structured, professional online classes are available for free, for example at www.Saylor.org, including testing and the issuance of a credential of completion. Thus a $30 fee is actually rather pricey. Perhaps the ultimate cost of general education online classes, including testing and accreditation, will be free or a few dollars. But the primary point here is that even charging $30 per online class and $150 for live workshops guided by mentor/masters still brings the total cost of a

forty-course undergraduate program down to $2,400—between 1/25th
and 1/50th the cost of a typical four-year undergraduate program.

Accreditation

Once we free the accreditation process from the cartel and let working
professionals design the curriculum in their specific field to align with
the state of the art and real-world enterprise needs, we open up a vast
spectrum of possible accrediting solutions and competing ideas.

As noted previously, a number of accreditation models are well-
established. The state bar exam for prospective lawyers essentially
bypasses the need for a diploma from a university; passing the bar exam
is the real-world accreditation. The same is true of other professions
such as architecture and engineering; the state licensing tests are
already issuing real-world accreditation, in effect making the
accreditation of coursework redundant.

Another model is the flight instructor, who takes the student through
real-world tests and grants accreditation based on the instructor's
experience and mastery. A flight instructor who passes an unqualified
candidate would soon lose his own reputation and license, and so the
system is self-regulating.

Another model for accreditation could simply be completing a project,
where, for example, a student must successfully complete ten workshop
projects to gain accreditation in digital fabrication.

There need not be one system or solution; it may well be that several
non-profit professional bodies each issue an accreditation process for
their field, and the ultimate victor is the process that wins the approval
of employers and working professionals. Any accreditation process (for
example, the current cartel one) that churns out graduates who are
unprepared for work in the emerging economy would be discounted by
employers and working professionals, and this competitive pressure
would reward the accreditation processes that accurately assess the
real-world knowledge base and skills of graduates.

Remaking Teaching/Learning and the Structure of Higher Education

We can now summarize how The Nearly Free University remakes teaching/learning (known professionally as pedagogy) and the structure of higher education.

You've probably noticed that I have toggled between present and future tense in describing the Nearly Free University model; this reflects the divide between the technological features of the model, which are already in use, and the structure of accrediting the student, which awaits future development and adoption. For simplicity's sake, this summary is in the present tense, as it describes a model that exists in the here and now.

1. The Nearly Free University is profoundly democratizing, as it demolishes artificial limits on access to curriculum and accreditation, and dismantles the Elitism and spoils system that has been protected by the cartel's artificial restrictions.

2. The open-source model of The Nearly Free University is also profoundly leveling economically and socially, as the opportunity to learn the key skills and mastery of a variety of subjects is open to all.

3. The Nearly Free University replaces the ineffective factory model of accrediting schools (a cartel system in which students are held hostage to an accreditation system that empowers the cartel rather than the student) with a model that accredits each individual via exams and other evidence of mastery designed by working professionals. This model effectively extends the accreditation template currently used for professions such as architecture and law to every student.

4. The Nearly Free University leverages the open-source curriculum of online lessons and courses so that the expertise and methodologies of the best instructors are available to all students. The coursework of 'learning to mastery' becomes transparent and flexible, so students can select the instructors and pathways that best suit their own learning styles and pace. The expertise is embodied in the systemized coursework and adaptive-learning software, which is constantly evolving in the open-source model.

5. The systemized coursework is designed and managed by working professionals in the field, assuring that the coursework relates directly to the real world of the emerging economy.

6. The Nearly Free University's core curriculum is not just general and applied knowledge but also the specific values and essential skills necessary to establish and maintain a livelihood in the emerging economy. The Nearly Free University recognizes that these values and skills are the incubator of human and social capital, the essential means of production in the emerging economy.

7. The Nearly Free University uses the workshop/laboratory model to instill these values and skills by producing value in real-world settings under the guidance of a working professional.

8. The Nearly Free University explicitly depends on transparency, voluntary collaboration and freely offered innovation to guide the evolution of coursework and accreditation. The professionalism of the NFU model flows not from a cartel Elite but from the open-source model.

9. The Nearly Free University attracts the best and the brightest not by offering tenured salaries but by offering the opportunity to have a profound impact on students' lives in a variety of ways, from recording brief lessons, providing full lecture courses, or mentoring students a few hours a week in workshops.

10. The Nearly Free University severs the legacy financial tie between costly research and the factory model curriculum. Research universities will be free to solicit funding from government and industry but these activities will no longer be funded by student tuition.

11. The administration of The Nearly Free University is largely automated and requires near-zero administrative overhead. Enrollment, payment, testing and accreditation are handled online and real-world workshops and proctored exams are administered online as well. The cost of workshops and proctored exams is reduced to the room rental fee, the hourly wage of the proctor or mentor, and the modest cost of server space and network administration. The NFU model is open to paid mentors/proctors

and to volunteers who choose to lower the cost of the curriculum and accreditation to near-zero.

12. Accreditation is understood to be a manifestation of human and social capital that is not a one-time event marked by the issuance of a diploma but instead a lifelong process of transparent collaborative verification by other professionals of the individual's mastery of applied skills and professional values.

13. The Nearly Free University explicitly embodies the systemic decentralization, transparency, adaptability and accountability that form the bedrock of the emerging economy. The NFU doesn't just prepare students for the emerging economy; it is an integral part of the emerging economy. As a result, the NFU is intrinsically less hierarchical and more reliant on big data analysis and the network intelligence of open-source, opt-in, self-organizing systems than the current higher education cartel. Crowdsourcing, collaboration and volunteerism are not just allowed on the margins; they are key infrastructures of the NFU.

14. The Nearly Free University is explicitly designed to operate and excel in a global era of financial, political and social tumult and transformation. The NFU manifests all the attributes of resilient systems:

    - a messy, fast-evolving structure that is flexible and highly responsive to changing industry needs,

    - a low cost of innovation,

    - a high bandwidth for collaboration,

    - a systemic tolerance for risk-taking and low-level volatility, and

    - a rapid uptake of the lessons learned from big data analysis and failure (the key slogan in this dynamic is "fail fast," i.e. learn quickly from failure and adapt to the lessons learned).

15. The existing higher education system is free to compete with the Nearly Free University, but once students are accredited individually, existing colleges will be operating without the protection of a cartel; instead they will be competing in a

transparent marketplace. This open competition to prepare students for individual accreditation and work in the emerging economy will improve the entire spectrum of higher education.

16. As the Elitist hierarchies that currently dominate the economy and society fray and fail, the value of a higher education passport stamp from an Elite university will lose ground to verifiable evidence of what the student can do in the real world. As referenced in Chapter 2, emerging economy enterprises such as Google are recognizing that mastering the process of obtaining a higher education stamp does not prepare the student for productive work in real economy. Indeed, those who skip the four-year stamping process for a skills-driven education are increasingly in demand for what they can accomplish in the real world.

17. The NFU model asks each student to calculate the cost in time and money of higher education and the real-world return on the investment of that time and money. Merely projecting old-economy trends is no longer an accurate guide to value e of a college degree in the emerging economy. An integral feature of the NFU model is the feedback loop between industries, employers, enterprises and mentors and the NFU curriculum, which is constantly evolving to serve the real-world needs of the work world.

Aligning the NFU Curriculum to the Emerging Economy

These are the key features of the emerging economy:

- What matters is what you can accomplish on your own and with others, not what stamps/degrees are on your higher education passport.

- The goal is to learn how to assemble ownership of human and social capital, which are the means of production in a knowledge economy.

- Careers in the emerging economy are ecosystems of collaboration and work.

To make sense of these points, we must first understand that we have entered a unique era of transformation comparable to the Industrial Revolution that radically transformed the global economy. Our economy is changing in profound ways, and the transformation will only gather speed.

The emerging economy is and will continue to be difficult to navigate, and many of us will look to our difficulty as a personal failure. The difficulty is systemic, and beyond individual decisions or policy adjustments. Existing systems unravel whether there is a replacement system in place or not.

The problems with the higher education industry are also systemic, and the current system will reset along with the entire economy and society. The question is whether the reset will serve the populace and the emerging economy, or if it will fail to do so.

To summarize: not only is higher education itself a failed system, it is serving a failed system. The inter-connected social, political and financial infrastructures of the status quo are unraveling for systemic reasons, and the task for those who grasp the profound nature of this obsolescence is to design an alternative infrastructure that is transparent, adaptable, decentralized and open equally to all. The Nearly Free University model is a key part of that new infrastructure.

PART TWO:
THE EMERGING ECONOMY

Chapter 3: Why the Current Economy Is Unsustainable

Given that the first purpose of education is to prepare the student to establish and maintain a productive livelihood, we first need to identify the key features of the emerging economy.

The emerging economy will of course share some characteristics with the economy of today, but it will also be a fundamentally different economy, as a result of seven world-changing dynamics.

1. The self-liquidation of the State-Cartel model

2. The exhaustion of the current model of global capitalism

3. The collapse of debt-based financialization

4. Labor-replacing technology

5. The demographics of an aging population

6. Resource depletion

7. The cultural contradictions of consumerist capitalism

8. The forces of Social Recession

Since I have addressed these topics in my books Why Things Are Falling Apart and What We Can Do About It and Resistance, Revolution, Liberation: A Model for Positive Change, I will only summarize the key points here.

If we sought to summarize the profound transformation ahead in two sentences, they would be:

1. The system of ever-expanding consumption, funded by ever-increasing debt, controlled by ever-greater centralization has reached negative returns and will collapse under its own weight. In other words, the interconnected financial, political and social infrastructures are unraveling as a result of their internal dynamics.

2. Wages are no longer an adequate model for distributing the surplus generated by the economy. The replacement of human labor by technology displaces paid work on such a large scale that employment by the government or the market economy will be unable to productively employ the labor force. As a result, paid

work will be scarce, not for business-cycle or political reasons, but for far deeper structural reasons.

This upends a social and economic system of distribution that stretches back to the beginning of modern capitalism in the 1300s. An economy in which labor is in permanent surplus and demand for labor is declining for technological and structural reasons is truly uncharted territory.

The U.S. economy is not immune to these eight forces, and as a result the nature of work and employment will change dramatically in the years and decades ahead. To prepare ourselves to successfully navigate the tumultuous era ahead, we must first understand how both the global and U.S. economies are being transformed.

Labor and Capital

Before we examine the six dynamics in detail, let's cover the fundamental components of every economy: labor and capital.

Labor and capital must generate a surplus. In other words, labor must generate a profit by generating goods and services that have a market value higher than total compensation costs, and capital must earn a positive return. Any enterprise that loses money will eventually use up its financial resources and go out of business.

This is not a feature of capitalism; it is a matter of physics. If output is less than input, the system breaks down once the capital (resources, energy, labor, financial capital) is exhausted.

An enterprise that earns a negative return (i.e. loses money) on either labor or capital invested is not sustainable.

Economies can mask this imbalance by subsidizing the loss with surplus taken from elsewhere in the system, but eventually the subsidy eats away the system's capital and the economy collapses.

To be productive in the marketplace, labor must generate a surplus. This surplus is necessary to pay the economy's social costs (funded via taxes) and to compensate the employer for the risk of investing in the enterprise. As an example, consider an oil producer. If oil is $100 per barrel, and the labor and cost of capital combined are $200 for every barrel of oil extracted and processed, the employer will soon go broke and close its doors, because the output is less than the input.

Not all labor is equally productive. Fast-food workers are working very hard to produce a large number of meals at a low price, but the surplus generated by their labor is relatively low, and so their wages and taxes are also relatively low.

A skilled oil-rig worker generates a hefty surplus (at least when oil prices are high) and so his/her wages and taxes are both high. Low-margin businesses have difficulty generating large surpluses; high-margin businesses (such as a technology company with gross profit margins of 40%) have a greater potential for generating large surpluses.

Societies depend on highly productive workers and enterprises to generate the surplus needed to fund the social costs: national defense, public health, protection of the environment, enforcing the rule of law, and so on. A nation with low-productivity workers and low profit-margin enterprises is poor. A nation with high-productivity workers and high profit-margin enterprises is wealthy (although that wealth may be squandered on mal-investment).

Highly productive people and enterprises generate wealth; this is known as wealth creation. Ultimately, surplus/wealth is what is left after the costs of production (inputs) are subtracted from revenues (output).

Society depends on the wealth being created to fund social costs. A low-productivity, low wealth-creation society cannot support a large government or extensive government services, for the fundamental reason that the economy doesn't generate enough surplus to support a large government.

The Pareto distribution discussed in Chapter 1 helps us understand why the top 5% of wage earners pay 60% of Federal income taxes, and the top 1% pay 38%. In terms of ownership of wealth, the top 10% own about 80% of all financial assets in the U.S. – thus demonstrating that wealth and wealth creation are concentrated, and as a result society depends to an extraordinary degree on those creating wealth to pay the social costs.

Extrapolating from this data, we conclude that for the education system to be effective at supporting the economy and society, it must foster highly productive individuals that have the values and skills to create highly productive enterprises. Without these highly productive people and enterprises, a society slips into poverty, regardless of its other merits or form of government.

Government has expanded in developed countries to dominate the economy and society. Roughly one-third to one-half of developed-economies' gross domestic product (GDP) is government (central, regional and local). The government is not just a regulatory body; it is central to the economy.

If the government pays its employees double what their labor is worth in the marketplace economy, this constitutes a transfer from one group with little organized political power (private-sector taxpayers) to a group with highly organized, well-funded political power (public employees). This subsidy acts as tax on the economy, as money that could have been invested productively is diverted to reward a politically favored group who are paid far more than their labor is worth in the open market. Eventually, this saps the economy of vitality as subsidies to favored groups or cartels reduce productive investment.

The key concept here is opportunity cost: if the government uses above-market labor to build a Bridge to Nowhere (that is, a bridge that serves a small and economically marginal populace, a project that was built as a political reward to a key cartel or constituency), this robs the economy of scarce capital that could have been invested far more productively (for example, a Bridge to Somewhere). As a result of the politically directed misallocation of capital, the Bridge to Somewhere doesn't get built.

Since we have lived through an unprecedented explosion of global trade and prosperity, many people naturally assume this ever-expanding wealth is a permanent feature of the global economy. For reasons we'll address in this chapter, this will not be the case. The current debt-based neofeudal model has run its course, and the next iteration of global capitalism, while sharing certain traits with past versions, will be structurally different.

What does wealth creation and opportunity cost have to do with education? If education is already unaffordable, then what will happen as wealth creation dries up? Secondly, if we are training our students for an economy of the past, our investment will be doubly misguided: the capital will have been malinvested and students will be ill-prepared for the emerging economy.

Labor's Declining Share of Value Creation

Those acquainted with Karl Marx's critique of capitalism will already be familiar with many aspects of this discussion of labor and capital.

What features of our economy are intrinsic to capitalism? One is private ownership of the means of production (as opposed to the government owning all wealth-producing assets) and the other is free-market competition for capital and labor.

By way of contrast, in a socialist system in which the government allocates all capital and labor, the competition for capital and wages is political, as the government rather than participants chooses which assets to invest in or liquidate and how much labor will be paid in wages.

The essence of capitalism can be outlined thusly:

1. Capital is placed at risk (invested) for an uncertain gain (profit).
2. The value of capital, credit, risk, resources, labor, goods and services are transparently discovered in an open market.
3. The market participants allocate capital and labor competitively as capital fluidly seeks the highest available return (profit) and labor seeks the highest wages/work satisfaction.
4. Capital must grow via profit or appreciation or it erodes from inflation and/or competition with more dynamic enterprises. (A fortune in buggy-whip manufacturing in 1901 vanished by 1920)
5. Innovation offers competitive advantages in transparent markets.

In an open market economy, highly profitable sectors attract capital seeking high returns. As competition expands production, the only way to increase profits is to lower production costs or establish a price-fixing cartel or monopoly that eliminates competition. In other words, competition fosters the fluid movement of capital and labor and reduces profits, which then drives the creation of cartels and monopolies that generate low-risk profits by limiting competition.

Let's turn to a real-world example. When I first visited China in 2000, that nation was suffering from a massive glut of television production: the capacity to manufacture TVs had expanded far beyond China's domestic demand for TVs. To wring out a profit in a highly competitive industry, manufacturers had to ramp up production while lowering the unit cost of labor (and thus the unit cost of each TV) to undercut the competition.

If an assembly line of 100 workers can produce 1,000 TVs a day, for example, the only ways to lower the price of the TV is to either lower the wages paid to the workers or invest capital in machinery that enables the same 100 workers to produce 2,000 TVs a day.

At 2,000 TVs a day, the per unit labor cost falls in half. At 1,000 TVs a day, the labor cost per TV might be $40. At 2,000 TVs per day assembled by the same 100 workers, the labor cost per unit drops to $20.

The key point here is that labor's share of the total production declines. If workers had taken home $1 million in wages to make 100,000 TVs at the old production rate of 1,000 TVs/day, they now take home $500,000 to make 100,000 TVs at the new production rate.

In other words, labor's share of value creation constantly declines as mechanization boosts productivity. It takes fewer workers to create the same value and profit.

This structural reduction in the need for labor leads to workers competing for scarce jobs. This competition tends to push wages lower, so workers face a double-whammy: their share of production relentlessly declines as productivity rises, and the downward pressure on wages constantly increases as the need for labor falls.

The competition to out-produce rivals with cheaper per-unit production costs and labor's competition for scarce jobs generates a structural crisis as both the cost per unit and the number of workers earning enough to buy the goods decline.

In practical terms, lowering the cost of the TV no longer sells units if the market is saturated or there are not enough workers with jobs to buy them.

Ironically, the modern central state has exacerbated this trend by imposing the inefficiencies of its favored cartels on employers and workers alike. Healthcare costs, for example, have risen dramatically, from less than 10% of the nation's economy (GDP) to almost 20%. In the classic diminishing returns generated by cartels, Americans' health is declining compared to our developed-world competitors, who provide healthcare to their citizens for 50% of what the U.S. spends per person.

Robots and software do not have skyrocketing healthcare costs, and so the pressure to replace high-cost labor with machines and software increases along with healthcare costs.

This is not theory; it is fact: according to the U.S. Department of Labor and the Bureau of Labor Statistics, labor's share of the U.S. economy has fallen steadily since 1981.

This contradiction is intrinsic to capitalism, as it results from competition and capital's need to earn a positive return.

State-Cartel Capitalism

The conventional way to maintain high returns on capital and maintain low-risk profit is to eradicate competition by whatever means available, and establish a cartel that controls supply and price.

Competition can be eradicated in a number of ways, but since the rise of the modern Central State, the lowest cost method has been to persuade the State to grant a monopoly or enable a cartel.

The key feature of state-cartel capitalism is that increases in price do not reflect an increase in value provided; they only reflect an increase in the rentier transfer of wealth from labor to the cartel. (Labor is simply those whose income is earned as opposed to those with unearned income from capital.)

The higher education cartel offers an excellent example. The State enforces the scarcity of accreditation and funds the cartel by issuing (and enforcing) student loans and taxpayer-funded grants. As noted in Chapter 1, the measurable value of the product (the curriculum and the diploma) has declined even as the price of a four-year degree has risen by over 500% when adjusted for inflation.

State-cartel capitalism has its own self-liquidating contradiction: the increasing transfer of wealth from labor to cartels and the State deprives households of income and bleeds the economy of capital that can be productively invested, while the state's expanding debts lead to a debt-spiral collapse.

Cartels have no incentive to improve their product; their primary incentive is to lobby the State to protect the cartel. Since the State protects and funds self-serving cartels, it oversees a vast misallocation of capital. In effect, the State allocates the nation's surplus to the unproductive cartels, robbing the nation of capital needed to invest in potentially productive assets.

To counter these diminishing returns, the State borrows and spends increasing sums of money, indenturing its productive citizenry to debt-serfdom as the costs of servicing the massive State debts rise.

In effect, state-cartel capitalism institutionalizes destructive incentives that lead to further concentration of wealth and power in the cartels and the State.

These intrinsic dynamics—the reduction of labor's share of value creation, and the concentration of wealth and power in cartels enforced by an increasingly debt-dependent State—lead to systemically destabilizing levels of inequality and debt.

The Terminal Phase of Global Capitalism 1.0

Two ideas dominate current economic theory and practice. The first is that economic activity expands and contracts in periodic but not entirely predictable cycles—what is known as the business cycle. The second is that these cycles can be smoothed into an uninterrupted permanent expansion by the fiscal and monetary policies of the central state (i.e. the central government) and the central bank (in the U.S., the Federal Reserve). Despite the many differences between European, Asian and American versions of capitalism, these ideas underpin all the modern state/bank policies, including those of nominally Communist China.

This notion of permanent state-managed expansion runs counter to two 19th/20th century schools of thought:

1. Marx's prediction (based on Hegel's concept of history) that increasingly disruptive crises of capitalism that would lead to its eventual collapse, and

2. the long wave cycles described by economists such as Nikolai Kondratieff (1892-1938) in which booms characterized by expansion of production capacity and credit are necessarily followed by busts in which the overcapacity is liquidated and impaired debt is renounced; this collapse of credit and debt results in a depression that clears the financial deadwood from the system, setting the stage for the next cycle of expansion.

French historian Fernand Braudel (1902-1985) sought to understand the history of capitalism from the ground up, so to speak, by first constructing a detailed map of the structures of everyday life—the title, as it happens, of Volume One (*The Structures of Everyday Life*) of Braudel's influential three-volume history, *Civilization & Capitalism, 15th to 18th Centuries*.

Braudel discerned a cyclical arc in the history of capitalism: history did indeed record long periods of expansion and contraction—extended booms and busts—but once the existing order fell into decay or crisis, the dominant model of capitalism was replaced by one with a wider global reach and increased capacity to accumulate capital.

Thus the dominant model of trade and finance in the 14th century that developed in the Italian city-states of Venice, Florence and Genoa was superseded by the Dutch model of global finance that was in turn superseded by the British Empire's territorial/military/financial model, which has been replaced by an American economic hegemony that is global without being based on a territorial empire.

In other words, beneath the never-ending cycle of boom-and-bust, there is a teleological path to global capitalism's expansion. This model of ever-larger systems of global dominance has been further developed by authors such as Giovanni Arrighi, author of *The Long Twentieth Century*, and American sociologist/theorist Immanual Wallerstein, whose world-system theory suggests that each expansion of capitalism arises from a new and more powerful world-system. A world-system is not a centralized territorial empire on the Roman model, but a complex network of diplomacy, military power, trade, credit and finance that dominates global capitalism.

This leads to a potentially vexing question: if America's centralized, financialized world-system already encompasses the entire globe, then how can any future world-system possibly expand beyond the present one? If the answer is that it cannot, then we are in the terminal stage of the current version of global capitalism that began roughly 700 years ago in the early 1300s. Capitalism will not expire, but a new iteration of decentralized, definancialized global capitalism will arise as the current version falls apart.

The Dynamics Undermining the Current System

Wallerstein identifies three long-term forces that are undermining capitalism's key function, the accumulation of more capital:

1. Urbanization, which increases the cost of labor.

2. Externalized costs (environmental damage and resource depletion) finally have to be paid.

3. Taxes increase as the central state responds to unlimited demands by citizens for more services (education, healthcare, etc.) and economic safety nets (pensions, welfare).

All three raise the cost of production and thus lower profit margins and the ability to accumulate capital.

China offers an excellent example of all three forces. As China's vast populace has moved in what some term the greatest migration in human history from rural villages to urban centers, wages have risen dramatically in response to an immense need for labor in factories. This has squeezed profits within China and pushed production to lower-cost inland cities. But given the long-term dynamic of rising urban wages, this is a temporary respite from higher wages.

In response to choking smog levels in Beijing and other Chinese cities, the government will increasingly be forced to pay the externalized costs of widespread pollution and environmental degradation. The only way the central state can pay these monumental costs is by raising taxes, further reducing profits and capital accumulation.

The influence of these three dynamics in the U.S. economy is easily traced. As wages rose and external costs came home to roost, the government imposed regulatory costs and taxes. Together these forces lowered profit margins. In response, capital moved production overseas to places like China with low wages, minimal environmental regulations and low taxes.

A fourth dynamic is what economist Joseph Schumpeter termed creative destruction, capitalism's need to clear the way for innovation by liquidating unproductive systems, enterprises and assets.

The need to liquidate impaired debt and unproductive assets is the heart of Kondratieff's insight into capitalism's key cycle. If financial deadwood is never cleared, it eventually chokes the system and leads to catastrophic financial firestorms of the sort which nearly brought down the global financial system in 2008.

Financialization

Braudel and Arrighi (among others) found that as profits from trade and production wither, capital migrates to finance-based rentier arrangements. Thus the merchant class of Venice responded to the decline of entrepreneurial trading profits by shifting capital to mainland agriculture and becoming an aristocracy that collected land rents from tenant farmers, i.e. a rentier class.

In other cases, capital flowed into finance: in broad terms, making money with financial dealings as opposed to investing in material production or trade. Though financial innovation is often presented as a recent phenomenon, the key characteristics of modern global finance were in operation by the early 1500's: stock and bond exchanges, hedging, joint stock ventures, highly profitable long-distance trade, commercial credit and central states funding their wars with private credit, to name just the top few.

Not coincidentally, financial innovation gave rise to spectacular speculative bubbles in assets ranging from tulips (1637) to trade monopolies (the Mississippi Company in 1719 and the South Sea Company in 1720).

From this perspective, the only innovation in the 2002-2008 boom and crash was the extension of the speculative bubble in dot-com and technology stocks to the asset class that forms the bedrock of wealth for two-thirds of American households, the family home.

In broad brush, this movement of capital from material production to finance greatly increases credit, leverage and speculation, the three basic tools of financialization. As a result, the economy and the government have both become increasingly dependent on ever-expanding debt. Financial profits have soared as a percentage of corporate profits, and the government has become dependent on massive borrowing to fund its basic programs.

The government has also become dependent on financial markets in two other ways: the rising stock market is held up as evidence of a robust economy and wise management by the central bank, and the government increasingly depends on financial profits to generate higher tax revenues.

If Kondratieff's insight into the cyclical nature of credit expansion and contraction is indeed fundamental to capitalism, we should expect to see a rapid rise in credit and a corresponding diminishing return on additional debt—precisely what we find. The economy's current modest growth is based on monumental increases in debt and money supply that are yielding ever-diminishing returns.

This trend is visible in Federal debt, which is tracing an exponential rise, and in the difference between the rates of growth in public and private debt and gross domestic product (GDP). Nominal GDP has climbed 60% since 2000, while debt has doubled (i.e. up 100%). By some analysts' calculations, it now takes $6 of additional debt to generate $1 of additional GDP. This is called debt saturation: additional borrowing no longer stimulates growth; it actually slows it, as an increasing share of borrowers' income must be devoted to paying interest on the rising debt. Other analysts conclude that the U.S. has already slipped into negative return on new debt: each additional $1 of debt no longer boosts GDP at all.

This is an example of diminishing return or marginal return: each unit of borrowed money yields less output than the previous unit. At some point, the cost of the borrowed money exceeds its yield, and borrowing more money actually reduces yield to a negative return.

If modest expansion is based on exponential increases in debt, that growth is not sustainable.

Relying on expanding debt to fuel growth has another deeply pernicious consequence: it transforms debtors into what I term debt-serfs, a reflection of the neofeudal nature of financialization. In a financialized economy, debt becomes the mechanism of servitude and obedience. People burdened with huge student loans, home mortgages and auto loans must obediently keep their nose to the grindstone to service their mountain of debt. Since the government is also borrowing heavily to fund its day-to-day programs, taxpayers are also debt-serfs, indentured by their government to service rapidly rising public debt.

There is yet another destructive feature of financialization's key dynamic of leveraging debt from a limited foundation of real-world collateral: credit is ultimately a claim on real-world resources and goods.

In our current fractional-reserve system, banks are able to create $25 of credit from every $1 in cash. This is the nature of fractional-reserve banking: the cash reserves are a fraction of the credit extended.

As a borrower, I might make a 20% cash down payment on a house, and borrow the other 80% on the basis of this cash collateral. In the case of unsecured credit such as student loans, I pledge future earnings as the collateral.

The person who has no access to credit can only buy goods and resources with his cash on hand; his ability to consume more is limited. The person with access to credit can buy many more goods; his ability to buy is only limited by his credit line. This means that the person with credit can buy far more goods and services than the person with cash, so credit is heavily incentivized in financialization.

The problem with this system of limited collateral/real-world resources and unlimited quantities of credit is that eventually the credit-money claims on resources far exceed the resources and the collateral, and the credit system implodes.

Thus financialization cripples the economy by incentivizing credit creation, borrowing and speculation. It concentrates financial wealth and misallocates capital on a grand scale, and indentures the citizenry to service ever-expanding private and public debts.

Centralization of Wealth and Power Corrupts Democracy

There is a political consequence to the extreme concentrations of financial wealth created by financialization. Concentrated wealth in a state-cartel economy is protected by the political machinery of the state. In a political system where increasingly costly elections are privately funded, concentrated wealth buys concentrated political power.

This feedback loop—concentrated wealth buys concentrated political power which is used to accumulate more wealth—corrupts democracy and the financial sector. Politicians respond to the pain felt by their major donors (the extremely wealthy), and regulatory agencies respond to the political pressure to protect the wealth of financial Elites. An example of this is the Too Big to Fail (TBTF) banks, which are neither investigated nor their frauds prosecuted, as they are viewed by the political establishment as indispensable to the nation's economy.

Moral hazard means that risk is disconnected from consequence: people and companies who have nothing to lose behave quite differently from those who might suffer losses. The government and Federal Reserve issued $23 trillion in backstops and guarantees to the financial sector in the wake of the 2008 meltdown. This created moral hazard, because the financial sector can now make huge bets and retain any profits, but if the bets sour, the government (and thus the taxpayers) absorbs the losses. This is known as privatizing profit and socializing losses.

Centralization of power and wealth corrupt the nation's political and financial systems by crippling the systems' self-correcting mechanisms. Instead of letting insolvent banks fail, the financier gamblers are rewarded and the taxpayers are punished. The nature of this corruption is corrosive: once the self-correcting mechanisms have been disabled, the system loses the ability to reform itself. Instead, we see simulacrum reforms, facsimiles that purport to correct the system but which actually perpetuate the predatory, parasitic financialization that has hollowed out the economy.

The Impact of Demographics

A rapidly aging workforce stresses the financial promises made by the State in three ways:

1. The expanding cohort of retirees increases government spending on pensions and healthcare;

2. The exit of productive older workers from the workforce reduces taxes derived from earned income, and

3. As retirees withdraw their savings from stocks and bonds and sell their empty-nest homes, these sales depress the market for stocks, bonds and housing.

In effect, the demographic demands on essentially open-ended government spending increase at the same time that tax revenues decline. Coupled with the reduced need for labor and declining yield on capital discussed earlier, current demographics lead to an unsustainable ratio of workers to retirees. In the U.S., the ratio of full-time wage earners to beneficiaries is already 1-to-1 (roughly 115 million workers to 110 million beneficiaries of Social Security, Medicare and Medicaid). This is in stark contrast to previous eras where the worker-beneficiary ratio was 16-to-1, or more recently, 3-to-1.

Few retirees are willing to accept less income and healthcare; rather, the default setting for humanity is to demand more income and healthcare. This sets up the impossible quandary of the State.

On a global scale, the key demographic trends are the rapid rise of the human population, and the parallel expansion of a resource-hungry middle class. As hundreds of millions of people have increased their earnings and disposable incomes, the global demand for energy, grain, metals and other commodities has skyrocketed. The easily accessible reserves of oil, fresh water and industrial metals have already been exploited, and as a result it now takes more energy and capital to extract each additional unit of resource. This calculation of return on investment is commonly known as energy returned on energy invested

(EROEI). As the easy-to-reach deposits of oil and ore are depleted, it takes more energy and capital to reach deeper, less accessible reserves.

It takes a certain amount of energy to produce anything, and as result energy is the most fundamental input of all production. In this sense, money is simply a measure of the cost of energy. If we understand money as ultimately being a measure of energy, then we can apply an EROEI-type analysis to all resources, not just oil but soil, fresh water, fertilizer, minerals and so on.

Superficially, it may seem Earth's resources are nearly limitless. Conventional analysts often issue grand pronouncements that the world isn't running out of oil, food production is expanding, seawater can be converted into fresh water, and so on. What these superficial claims fail to account for is the declining return on energy and capital invested: it takes enormous quantities of energy and capital to extract and process unconventional oil and other natural resources, and there is a diminishing return for each unit of energy and capital invested. Furthermore, many resources are being depleted that cannot be restored or replaced at any cost - for example, fresh water aquifers, soil and ocean fisheries.

The demand of an expanding global middle class for more resource-intensive goods and services requires enormous investments of energy and capital to sustain. As a result, costs of production will rise as the costs of extraction and processing conventional sources rise.

Unconventional energy sources may replace increasingly costly conventional sources, but such alternatives are on the margins of global supply and demand, and are decades away from replacing conventionally extracted supplies.

Headlines declaring the current abundance of natural gas, for example, fail to note that even unlimited natural gas cannot replace what has already been depleted: ocean fisheries, fresh water reservoirs, topsoil and easily accessible deposits of oil and minerals.

The Impossible Quandary of the State

In an idealized capitalist economy, the government's primary function is to act as a neutral referee as markets transparently discover the price of capital, credit, labor, goods, services and risk. However, in the real world, the government has an entirely different agenda: protecting privately owned cartels.

We have seen how unfettered competition leads to lower returns on capital, leaving a decreased amount of surplus for the government to collect in taxes. Competition lowers profits, protecting cartels from competition increases profits. The government's own self-interest requires enforcing quasi-monopolies and cartels as a means of producing enough private surpluses to support the government.

In earlier times and iterations of global capitalism, the trading company was the preferred form of quasi-monopoly: the government granted exclusive privileges to trading companies in return for a share of the vast profits that accrued.

This is the key dynamic of state-cartel capitalism: the state enables quasi-monopolistic profits which then support the state's own expansion. A low-profit margin economy cannot generate enough surpluses to support a vast state, and this explains the state's role in suppressing competition in favor of cartels. Examples include the U.S. government's protection of cartels in its bloated, inefficient healthcare system and China's protection of equally bloated and inefficient state-owned enterprises (SOEs). This state protection of quasi-monopolies feeds a politically dominant financial aristocracy.

The state enforces this transfer of wealth to cartels via a number of mechanisms, each of which acts as a tax on the economy. These mechanisms are generally well-hidden. For example, the state creates obscure regulatory barriers to competitors and complex tax shelters for politically favored industries. This enables cartels to maintain high prices and profits and the State to continue to collect taxes.

There is an ironic feedback to this dynamic. As competition in productive sectors lowers profit margins, there are fewer surpluses available to subsidize the protected cartels. Freed from exposure to market pressures, the state and the cartels become increasingly inefficient: their costs rise while the value of their output declines.

Subsidizing the inefficient sectors bleeds capital from the productive sectors, starving them of investment and weakening their ability to generate gains in productivity. As their margins shrink and the state-cartel expenses rise, the two trends feed each other in a self-reinforcing feedback loop. At some point, the productive sectors can no longer support the inefficient state-cartel sector.

State-enabled bank and cartel profits are skimmed at the expense of labor and households. China is an extreme example: the household/consumer sector is a meager 34% of China's economy. In the U.S., corporate profits set new highs while household income (adjusted for inflation) has declined 8% since 2008.

This dynamic of diverting surplus from households to state-cartels increases wealth disparity, which raises the risk of social instability that threatens the political Elites. The state must fulfill the demands of its people or face destabilizing social unrest.

As a result, the state has two competing core mandates: it must enforce private quasi-monopolies to generate the profits it needs to fund its own expansion, and it must satisfy enough of its citizenry's demands for financial security to provide political stability. If the state fails to maintain quasi-monopolistic cartels, profit margins plummet and private capital is unable to fund taxes, investment and jobs; the economy spirals down as investment and capital accumulation stagnate. If the state fails to meet the demands of its citizenry for more social services and income security, it risks being replaced or overthrown.

This is the nation-state's quandary everywhere. With growth slowing and parasitic cartels increasingly costly to maintain, the State has difficulty funding its ever-expanding social spending. In response, the State raises taxes and borrows the difference between its ever-rising spending and its stagnant revenues. The State's rising debt further squeezes spending as the interest on the debt rises.

Central banks have resolved this by printing vast sums of money and creating even vaster sums of credit which are pumped into the economy in the vain hope that the money will not be malinvested or used to inflate yet another short-lived asset bubble. Some of this central bank money is used to buy government debt (bonds), keeping interest rates low and enabling the state to borrow gargantuan sums without having to worry about any bond market discipline.

This expansion is not limited to struggling developed nations. China's money supply has risen by 35% in a mere two years, far outpacing its relatively modest growth in output.

In other words, debt saturation applies to national governments. Once monumental doses of new debt-based spending no longer stimulate growth, servicing the interest on the expanding debt cripples the government's ability to fund its social spending and support politically powerful cartels.

Something has to give, but whatever gives will collapse the government's finances and the economy. There is no way out of this quandary.

The Digital Revolution's Impact on Labor and Profits

Global capital is finding its input costs rising on virtually every front: energy and resources cost more, externalized costs are coming home to roost, urbanized labor demands higher wages and benefits, and the State is raising taxes to fulfill its increasingly costly promises.

As a result of rapid progress in robotics and networked software, it is increasingly cheaper and more productive to replace human labor with machine and digital capital. This includes digital fabrication (also known as 3-D printing), robotics, software, and Internet-based communication/social media applications.

This has a number of poorly understood consequences. We already noted that reducing labor's share of value creation reduces the total wages available for consumption and taxes. This cripples the consumer-based economy and severely restricts the state's ability to raise payroll and consumption-based taxes.

Since central banks are flooding the global economy with cheap credit, the capital needed to enter profitable markets is readily available. As a result, competition, capacity and output all increase. As products and services that can be produced by robots and software becomes increasingly abundant, supply exceeds demand and profit margins shrink.

In a world of rising competition and near-zero interest rates, it makes sense for corporations to use low-cost credit to buy machines and software to reduce the number of human employees. As robotics and software decline in cost, the cost of payroll taxes, healthcare and pensions continues to rise, increasing the incentives to replace human labor wherever possible.

As the capabilities of machines and software expand, an increasing number of human-labor tasks can be automated. The tasks that can be automated are not limited to low-skill assembly; white-collar work that is the bedrock of middle-class incomes is being exposed to the same forces that replaced agricultural and industrial labor in the 20th century.

With less income going to labor, demand for goods declines, further exacerbating the gap between capacity (rising) and demand (declining). This low-return environment generates less profit available to invest in future production, and the highest return on investment is increasingly political lobbying/bribery to lock in profits from state-enabled cartels.

However, we have seen that state-protected cartels are the least efficient sectors of the economy, and over time their share of the national income crowds out more productive spending. In the U.S., the healthcare cartels now absorb about 18% of the nation's GDP; on a per capita basis, the U.S. spends roughly twice as much as our developed-world competitors on healthcare, even as millions of Americans lack coverage and government healthcare program costs expand at rates well above the growth of the underlying economy.

Simply put, government-protected cartels crowd out productive investment and this misallocation of capital eventually bankrupts the nation.

The Cultural Contradictions of Consumerist Capitalism

The central narrative of global capitalism 1.0 is that prosperity can only expand if there is more of everything—what we call growth. The driver of growth is consumption, and thus expanding consumption by any means necessary is the goal of the state and central bank.

This narrative is a belief structure, and like many other belief structures, we take it for granted that it is true, or at least supported by evidence. But like most other cultural contexts, it is largely unexamined: the growth via consumerism narrative is simply accepted in much the same way that the structure of feudalism was accepted as the only possible way to live in 11th century Europe or Japan. Though we now know this assumption was false, to those living in the 11th century it was the natural order of life. Psychiatrist and author R.D. Laing observed that what is obvious to us is not at all obvious when viewed from an outside context or with the benefit of history.

If we examine our beliefs about growth and consumerism rather than simply accept it as the bedrock of our current way of life, we find that its core assumption—consumerist excess creates wealth, prosperity and happiness—is false. There are two cultural contradictions at the very heart of the consumerist ideology that help us understand its profound economic and social failure:

1. The consumerist society's relentless focus on the essential project of consumerism, which is the only self that is real is the self that is purchased and projected, creates a culture of narcissism. Consumerism rests on the implicit belief that our real self can only be expressed by owning and displaying signifiers of social status. If we do not possess these signifiers, we are a non-entity, stripped of self-worth and identity.

    Christopher Lasch's 1979 book *The Culture of Narcissism: American Life in an Age of Diminishing Expectations* zeroed in on the essence of this narcissism: a fear of the emptiness that lies at the very core of consumerism.

    The narcissism bred by consumerism nurtures a deep emotional isolation and immaturity, what I term permanent adolescence, which leaves many young people without the tools needed to handle criticism, collaboration and the pressures of the workplace.

    What the consumerist ideology actually creates are alienation, social atomization, self-absorption, and a profound contradiction at the heart of the consumerist model of endless growth: the narcissism that powers consumerist desire is at odds with the demands of the workplace that generates the income needed to consume.

2. Sociologist Daniel Bell's 1988 book, *The Cultural Contradictions of Capitalism*, laid out the contradiction at the heart of all consumerist

cultures: such cultures generate an unquenchable need among successful people for ever-expanding personal gratification, but this need undermines the work ethic that led to their financial success.

If we combine these two analyses, we find the narcissism that results from the focus on personal gratification undermines the person's ability to function effectively in the workplace. Personal gratification encourages self-absorption even as it erodes authentic identity and the resilience which enables emotional growth—the essential characteristic of adulthood. If there is any personality that is unsuited for the emerging economy workplace, it is the narcissistic consumer—the very type of person that our consumption-driven economy creates and nurtures.

Ironically, the flattening of corporate management structures and the demands for higher interpersonal skillsets has eroded the security provided by the top-down hierarchy of previous eras. Instead of working fewer hours and doing easier work—the implicit promise of ever-expanding prosperity—work is becoming more challenging and insecure even as compensation declines.

Japan is the first developed economy to enter the final phase of financialization and state-cartel management of the economy. Japan's economy has been stagnant for over 20 years, and its political and financial Elites are pursuing a policy of doing more of what has failed spectacularly: ramping up debt, financialization and state-cartel manipulation of financial markets. The end result will be a collapse of the very system they are trying to restart.

No wonder Japan's Lost Generations are mired in narcissism: not only are expectations of secure, high-income jobs diminished, the work is more demanding and the security and pay are too low to support the consumerist lifestyle that their society has implicitly promised everyone who goes to college and works hard. This is the direct consequence of the supremacy of a consumerism that is dependent on financialization.

An economy dependent on debt-fueled consumption is one that will necessarily implode from its internal contradictions: debt and leverage eventually exceed the value of the underlying collateral and the nation's ability to service that debt, and the narcissism of consumerism leads to social recession, a crippling state of dispiriting stagnation that breeds insecurity, frustration and unhappiness.

The ultimate contradiction in our debt-fueled consumption economy is this: how can an economy have endless growth when wages and opportunities for secure, high-paying jobs are relentlessly declining for structural reasons while debt and interest costs inexorably expand? It cannot. Financialization, consumerist narcissism and the end of the endless growth model are inextricably linked.

The Forces of Social Recession

The term social recession has two distinct meanings: a handful of social scientists began using the term over a decade ago to describe the erosion of social cohesion that results from the decline of institutions such as marriage and the rise of social problems such as teen pregnancy.

I use social recession to describe a different phenomenon, the social and cultural consequences of permanently recessionary economies such as Japan, Europe and the U.S.

These ten conditions characterize social recession:

1. High expectations of endless rising prosperity have been instilled in generations of citizens as a birthright.

2. Part-time and unemployed people are marginalized, not just financially but socially.

3. Widening income/wealth disparity as those in the top 10% pull away from the shrinking middle class.

4. A systemic decline in social/economic mobility as it becomes increasingly difficult to move from dependence on the state (welfare) or parents to the middle class.

5. A widening disconnect between higher education and employment: a college/university degree no longer guarantees a stable, good-paying job.

6. A failure in the status quo institutions and mainstream media to recognize social recession as a reality.

7. A systemic failure of imagination within state and private-sector institutions on how to address social recession issues.

8. The abandonment of middle class aspirations by the generations ensnared by the social recession: young people no longer aspire to (or cannot afford) consumerist status symbols such as autos.

9. A generational abandonment of marriage, families and independent households as these are no longer affordable to those with part-time or unstable employment, i.e. the "end of work".

10. A loss of hope in the young generations as a result of the above conditions.

Social recession results from the confluence of three dynamics: definancialization, the demise of growth-positive demographics and the devolution of the consumerist model of endless growth, where growth is defined as consuming more resources and services.

The narcissism bred by consumerism has nurtured a kind of emotional isolation and immaturity (permanent adolescence), which leaves many young people without the tools needed to handle criticism, collaboration and the pressures of the workplace.

Social Recession is thus a complex phenomenon that affects both the psychology of individuals and the overall economy and society. Trapped in a post-growth economy that offers diminishing opportunities to earn enough to meet the high aspirations of the dominant consumerist ideology, young people surrender aspirations for marriage, a household of their own and children.

A relative few make it onto a traditional professional, corporate or government career path, and everyone else is left in part-time suspended animation with few options for adult expression or development.

The systemic inability of the status quo to offer a future that includes marriage, ownership of assets and family to everyone left out of the top earners leads to a profound social and individual stagnation. The next iteration of global capitalism must provide a spectrum of opportunities for non-consumerist prosperity for everyone willing to contribute, not just the professional and financier classes.

Chapter 4: The Terminal Phase of the Old Order

We now understand the structural forces that are causing the social, political and financial infrastructures of the status quo to come apart at the seams. This process of the existing order collapsing under its own weight and the emergence of a new set of infrastructures is the cycle of history; we can trace similar periods of systemic transition back to the Bronze Age giving way to the Iron Age circa 500 B.C.E. More recent examples include the shift from feudalism to nascent modern capitalism and the transition from the first phase of the Industrial Revolution to the current iteration of global capitalism.

These transitional eras are always messy because the old system frays and breaks down long before the new set of infrastructures has matured. For reasons we will discuss in this chapter, participants cling fiercely to the current system even as it is undeniably failing. This human desire to conserve the perquisites of the present system despite its obvious failure actually hastens the process of collapse, as reforms are limited by the need to maintain the perquisites of current beneficiaries. Superficial reforms inevitably fail and much of what was considered absolute melts away.

The emergence of new financial, political and social infrastructures is equally messy, as the process is one of trial-and-error and conflict between competing models. If existing models still worked, there would be no need for new systems. But since the existing models are failing, they provide little guidance in assembling new models.

The transition from the Bronze Age to the Iron Age took about 200 years, reflecting the difficulties in that era of recording and distributing innovations. The transition from the feudal order to modern capitalism was also lengthy and disruptive. In our current Internet Age, the ease of recording and distributing disruptive innovations will greatly speed the process of dissolution and the evolution of new infrastructures.

The key characteristics of our current system are centralization, the pre-eminence of credit and finance and the distribution of surplus via wages. These are precisely the features that have reached diminishing returns and are collapsing. That the present status quo has very little to offer the future characterizes major transitions.

Economic Darwinism

Just as natural selection selects for traits that improve the odds of success/survival in the natural world, Economic Darwinism advances people and policies that boost profits and power within the dominant financial environment. The more extreme the environment, the greater the rewards offered for extreme adaptations.

In a hyper-financialized environment of near-zero interest and abundant credit, people and enterprises that make massive, high-risk bets reap extreme rewards. Those who exhibited prudence were weeded out, as their caution yielded poor returns. Those willing to make the riskiest bets were rewarded with the largest returns, and their success pushed them to the top of the leadership pyramid.

But once the environment changes from one that rewards risk to one that rewards prudence, the people who moved up to the top in the previous era are the worst possible choices for leadership, as the traits that enable successful management of credit-risk crises have been selected out of the system.

As analyst Brenton Smith (no relation) explained in his online essay *The One Phrase That Explains the Great Recession*, "The Federal Reserve's 20-year policy of easy money created an environment virtually assured to select bankers, bureaucrats, educators, and elected officials who least understood the consequences of a credit crisis." During speculative credit booms, Smith noted, "The statistical likelihood of any system promoting someone with a sensible risk perspective becomes lower and lower."

Smith explained the key dynamic thusly: "Capitalism acts as a steroid, drawing cash into successful companies. This process encourages other companies to emulate the practices that made certain companies successful."

Economic Darwinism puts selective pressure not just on enterprises but on individuals and policies, which together form a self-reinforcing system: those best adapted to profit in eras of speculative credit expansion gain political and financial power which is used to further extend the environment of financial excess. The policies that enabled the enormous success of financialization also gain influence, furthering the careers of those who pushed them.

Success in Wall Street leads to influence in Washington D.C., and this feeds an incestuous revolving-door between centers of political and financial power.

The irony of Economic Darwinism is that outsized success in extreme environments such as financialization selects leadership, policies and institutions that will necessarily fail spectacularly once the environment changes. Here is Smith's apt description of the result: "The boom times enabled animals called bankers to grow to massive size. Nature selected those who were the fittest for that environment. When the environment changed, these animals were like dinosaurs staring at the glaciers."

Our leadership, policies, mindset and institutions are all dinosaurs staring at the advancing glaciers of a completely different era for which they are uniquely ill-adapted to survive.

The Erosion of Community by the State

The economy and society are composed of three interwoven elements: community, the marketplace, and government. In the U.S., community is comprised of neighborhood groups, churches, not-for-profit associations, etc.—any voluntary organization that is not funded by the state (government) or engaged in for-profit activity as its primary purpose. The community and the marketplace are typically self-organizing, and they arise in virtually all human societies. In contrast, government (the state) is centralized and has a formal structure.

For the purposes of this overview, the key dynamic is that in advanced nations, the community has a limited role in the economy. The marketplace of wages, labor, enterprise, credit and capital is regulated by the state, which collects taxes and constitutes between a third and one-half the economy. This is in contrast to developing nations, where up to 90% of the economic activity occurs in the community-based economy of barter and informal, unregulated trade. In developed nations, this activity is viewed as an illegal black-market; the state demands that all economic activity be conducted within its sphere of control and taxation.

While the rise of the state has reduced the community's role in the economy and society, market forces have centralized much of what was once decentralized and local. Globalization of trade and the rise of corporations that harness vast economies of scale have replaced much of the informal economy's production with mass-produced and mass-marketed goods. The net result of this erosion of the informal economy is that residents in developed nations must have a significant cash-money income to survive, and if they are unable to earn that income in the formal market economy, there are few alternatives other than becoming a state dependent, i.e. drawing payments and subsidies from the government.

We can understand the difference by considering what happens to an urban worker who loses his job. In developed nations, the worker must find an income soon, either from a job or a payment from the state. In a developing nation, the worker can always go return to the village and eke out a livelihood in the community-based economy. In developed nations, those who are unable to earn wages in the market economy are dependent on the state for their livelihood. This includes pensioners, single parents without a wage income, the unemployed and the disabled.

In eras of economic contraction, an increasing number of able-bodied adults become dependent on the state for their income. This dependence can quickly transition from a temporary arrangement to a culture of dependence. This creates a number of follow-on problems.

One is that the state's expenditures rise significantly, forcing the state to borrow more money (i.e. increase deficit spending) and/or raise taxes, pulling money away from private investment and consumption. But the more pernicious problem arises on the individual level.

On the surface, it may seem that dependents should be happy because the state supplies their needs and they are free of the burden of competing in the marketplace for jobs. But dependence on the state has several hidden costs. Self-worth is based on autonomy, self-reliance and a productive role in society. The dependent has none of these sources of identity and self-esteem, and as a result is prone to depression and an unhealthy focus on perceived injustices. With the state essentially paying the person to withdraw from the marketplace, the dependent eventually loses the skills and self-confidence needed to re-enter the job market. Dependence has eroded his ability to accept risk, make realistic assessments and persevere in the face of setbacks.

There is another negative consequence of dependence on the state. When an individual receives cash from the government, he no longer needs other people's cooperation to earn his livelihood: all his basic material needs are now met by the state. He withdraws into a distorted world without reciprocity; he is free to indulge in unproductive pastimes and has no incentive to concern himself with the needs of others. The most important relationship in his life is his tie to the state because it is the source of his income. The state's payment has effectively isolated him from the community because he no longer needs to contribute to the community to earn his keep. He is alienated from the productive world and cut off from positive sources of self-worth and meaning.

In this way, state payments to working-age individuals destroy community, self-reliance and self-confidence. Dependence erodes the individual's ability to be productive in the real world—the foundation of self-worth and a meaningful life—their hope for the future and the resilience of the overall economy.

The Erosion of Institutional Purpose and Effectiveness

There is a critical dynamic within the sprawling, politically protected bureaucracies that dominate our economy and society that can be traced back to the Roman Empire's decline and fall: institutions have an innate tendency to expand even as they lose sight of their real function. If the function is complex and the political protection strong, momentum and self-interest provide institutional purpose even as the institution fails to deliver its original function.

Individual contributions and institutional success are both difficult to measure in large bureaucracies, and it is tempting to define success by easily achieved metrics that reflect positively on the management. As the organization loses focus on its original purpose, personal aggrandizement and advancement tend to become the focus of

117

departments and individuals. The core purpose of the institution is still given lip service but gets replaced with facsimiles of managerial expertise and bureaucratic infighting over resources. Easily gamed metrics get substituted for actual success.

As noted previously, people who have no skin in the game behave quite differently from those who face consequences (i.e. moral hazard). Bureaucracies tend to institutionalize moral hazard: those managing the institution's departments rarely suffer any personal consequence when the institution fails to perform. Funds are spent, but the individuals managing the institution's budget suffer no losses should their policies result in failure.

By breaking the institutional purpose into small pieces, with the success of each measured by easily reached targets, the institution can be failing its overall function even as every department reports continued success in meeting its goals. Repeated failure and loss of focus erode the institution even as those in charge advance up the administrative ladder.

The disconnection between the failure to fulfill the institution's original function and the leadership's rise feeds cynicism in the institution's employees and erodes their initiative. Soon the institutional culture is one of self-aggrandizement, gaming of departmental targets, protection of budgets and a collapse of the work ethic to the minimum level needed to avoid dismissal and lock in hefty pensions.

Dissolution of Accountability and the Diversion of Responsibility

Centralization in all its forms has two other destructive dynamics: accountability is dispersed and individual responsibility is diverted.

In theory, centralization concentrates accountability, but in practice, actual accountability is passed down the hierarchy to the level with the least control and power, to those with insufficient power to fix what's broken. Accountability becomes a charade of passing legitimate accountability down the hierarchy to someone else. In this fashion organizational and individual accountability is lost.

One way organizations shirk accountability is to divert responsibility for their failings to external causes rather the real causes, which reside in the organization itself. The classic example is "we need more money to fix what's broken." Despite the lack of examples where an increase in budget actually resolved the organization's ineffectiveness, this is the first diversion pursued by almost every organization regardless of its size.

Such diversions are all variations on the old "the dog ate my homework" excuse: some force beyond our control is rendering us ineffective. With a larger budget and staff, we might make some headway.

Since staff levels and budgets are not the real source of the organization's failings, adding staff and funding do not fix what's broken. Instead, they hasten the implosion of the organization as its dysfunctions remain unaddressed.

Consumption, Investment, Interest and Opportunity Cost

The dynamic between investment and productivity is absolutely critical to understanding why the state-cartel debtocracy is doomed to stagnation and eventual reset.

The only way to increase value, surplus, wealth and capital accumulation is by increasing productivity or lowering input costs. Leveraging debt to fund speculation (financialization) and funding consumption with debt (debt-serfdom) cannot boost productivity, as speculation and consumption both drain capital from productive investment. Taxing the most productive sectors of the economy to subsidize the least efficient sectors also diverts capital from productive to unproductive spending.

Simply put, an economy that spends its scarce capital on consumption, debt service, speculative malinvestments and subsidies to the least productive sectors will become poorer.

The only way to sustainably boost wages is to increase productivity. An economy that incentivizes consumption, debt, malinvestment and subsidies of politically favored cartels will be unable to fund productive investment, and as a result average wages in that economy will tend to decline.

Relying on debt to fund consumption has a particularly pernicious long-term consequence: debt must be serviced, i.e. interest must be paid until the debt is retired (paid off) or renounced (defaulted).

If we spend cash on consumption, that reduces the pool of capital available to invest in future productivity. That is bad enough, but when we borrow money to fund consumption, we have to pay interest on that debt far into the future—in the case of state borrowing, future taxpayers will be paying interest essentially forever. These interest payments take money away from both consumption and investment, lowering both the standard of living and the investment needed to increase productivity. If we add up the total cost of the debt service, debt-based consumption costs far more than its initial price.

There is an additional cost to consuming rather than investing: opportunity cost. As noted in Chapter 1, if we build a Bridge to Nowhere, the opportunity cost of that decision is that we no longer have the capital to build a Bridge to Somewhere.

If we keep borrowing money and squandering it on malinvestments and consumption, our income declines for two reasons: productive investments are starved by interest payments, which leads to falling real wages, and then we have less to spend/invest as the interest rises along with the debt.

Politicians seeking votes and Keynesian economists both confuse consumption and investment. Housing, infrastructure and higher education are all touted as investments, yet much of the spending on these is actually consumption.

A sprawling McMansion in the middle of nowhere is touted as an investment, but it is actually a form of consumption. A Bridge to Nowhere is consumption. A college degree that offers a near-zero employment premium in the real economy is also consumption.

Keynesian economists believe that demand for more goods and services—in other words, consumption—is the cure for all economic ailments. I term the Keynesians a Cargo Cult, as their worship of consumer demand leads to a magical-thinking faith that more consumption will magically increase productivity and thus prosperity.

Buying low-quality particle-board shelving from China is consumption, but it does not magically increase productivity in America. Rather, it introduces a steep opportunity cost, as that money could have been invested in a productive asset or at least a locally made higher-quality item that would not end up in the landfill.

The Keynesian Cargo Cult makes matters even worse by promoting debt-based consumption by both the private sector and the state. As described above, borrowing money to fund consumption leads not to rising prosperity but to the impoverishment of declining income and productive investment.

The Keynesian Cargo Cult's emphasis on increasing consumption by increasing debt leads to asset bubbles, misallocation of capital and rising debt loads. Any spurt of growth from such central-planning interventions is unsustainable, and establishes incentives that lead to deeper crashes and distortions. In fact, if you set out to design an economic policy that would inevitably lead to catastrophic collapse, it would be the Keynesian School's support of neofeudal, neocolonial financialization as the key driver of growth in a policy that encourages rising debt and leveraged speculation.

All the incentives of Keynesian policy favor increasing debt, misallocation of capital and unproductive consumption, and all the disincentives weaken investments in productivity and capitalism's creative destruction of malinvestments.

The Keynesian Cargo Cult's beliefs and policies can be summarized as follows:

1. Growth arises from increasing consumption funded by debt.

   (This is false. Growth based on using borrowed money for consumption does not increase productivity and has high opportunity costs.)

2. Virtually any spending on housing, higher education, healthcare and national defense is an investment.

   (This is also false. Most of this spending is consumption, as it does little to boost productivity.)

3. The cost of servicing debt that was borrowed to fuel consumption is modest and has no ill effects once the economy starts growing again.

(This too is false. Value, wealth and income only increase if productivity increases, and debt-based consumption does not boost productivity. Therefore, an economy based on borrowing money for consumption cannot grow; it can only inflate asset bubbles that generate phantom collateral, assets that quickly revert to their pre-bubble valuations once the speculative bubble pops. Rising interest payments reduce the national income available for productive investment and future consumption, thereby leading to lower incomes and general impoverishment.)

Complexity, Gatekeeping, and Other Rentier Arrangements

In broad brush, the state either encourages productive investment and transparent competition or it discourages them in favor of supporting politically protected cartels and fiefdoms. Such support boils down to what are known as rentier arrangements. The classic rentier arrangement is feudalism, where the landowner collects rents from serfs who are indentured to the estate. The landowner collects the surplus from the serfs' labor without creating any value himself.

The modern version of this relationship, neofeudalism, operates in more subtle ways. In general, debt is the mechanism of servitude in the current economy: the household with a large home mortgage, student debt, and auto loan and credit card debt is effectively indentured to the banks, which skim the surplus of the household's labor. (Recall that the banks can borrow money from the Federal Reserve at near-zero interest, so they have a massive subsidy from the state when they issue loans to households.)

Complexity is another rentier arrangement. There are two kinds of complexity: self-organizing (e.g. the Internet), and institutional (e.g. the thousands of pages of Federal tax code).

Institutional complexity—for example, complicated tax codes add costs but provide no increase in productivity—act as complexity moats, defending state-protected fiefdoms and cartels. Were income taxes eliminated in favor of consumption taxes collected at the point of sale, a vast parasitic industry of tax preparation and loophole exploitation would vanish, freeing immense sums of capital for productive investment.

Complexity also acts as a rentier arrangement, as everyone doing business has to pay what amounts to a rent to have their papers processed. Developing-economy kleptocracies excel at these sorts of official rentier arrangements: there is a fee (and often a bribe as well) to have your papers stamped, and there are inevitably a large number of stamps required, but no real value added anywhere along the line.

In the U.S., these rentier arrangements are wrapped very prettily as higher education, public safety or environmental protection or other equally positive-sounding projects. But the actual arrangement has very little to do with the purported purpose. Even when the process has a yield, it is a marginal return. Environmental review is a common example. Like Mom, apple pie, education and national defense, no one can possibly be against environmental protection. But the yield on a costly environmental review of every small lot in an urban zone may be marginal. Further increasing the cost is the cumbersome process, which enables any not in my backyard (NIMBY) critic to pour sand in the gears with potentially no gain in environmental protection whatsoever.

Large-scale development of environmentally sensitive wetlands is another matter—a careful review of the environmental impact of large developments is commonsense. But when the process is applied to every project, regardless of its potential environmental impact, it becomes a rentier arrangement where the consultants and state agencies skim a fee in the same manner as the developing world kleptocrat.

Gatekeeping is another rentier arrangement. As in the example above, if you need your papers stamped to move forward, you must pay the gatekeeper, even if they add no value to the economy. Since a college degree is seen as having one's papers stamped for entry into a more expansive job market, this is the acme of a rentier arrangement.

The Terminal Phase of Debt Expansion, Consumerism and State-Cartel Capitalism

Clearly, we've reached the terminal phase of financialization and dependence on debt to fuel expansion. Just as clearly, diminishing returns on capital and the reduction of labor's share of the national income are threatening the consumerist foundations of global capitalism and state finances.

It's critical that we understand the dynamics of Economic Darwinism, lower capital accumulation and systemic misallocation of capital, for only then can we understand why reforms are incapable of reversing the processes that have undermined state-cartel capitalism.

We also must grasp that the traditional understanding of capital and labor no longer describes the dynamics of the emerging economy. Low-skilled labor simply doesn't generate value and surplus (i.e. productivity and profits) to the degree it once did. The decline of labor's share of the national income (already painfully visible in statistics) is not an aberration; it is a structural trend. This decline in labor's share of output undermines the foundation of the consumer-debt based economy, and our beliefs about labor's role in producing output and surplus. As noted at the beginning of this chapter, it also undermines the entire system of distributing the economy's surplus via wages, which in turn undermines consumption, taxes and government finances.

If cartels have stunted the economy's capacity to accumulate capital and allocate it productively, the state will be unable to sustain its protection of the cartels and its social spending.

On an even larger scale, the longstanding trend of centralizing power and control as a means of reaping the efficiences of economies of scale is also crumbling. Financialized centralization has resulted in sclerotic, inefficient institutions riddled with moral hazard and ruled by self-serving, politically protected Elites. This is the core of what I call neofeudalism, as politically protected cartels and state fiefdoms are ruled by what amounts to a financial-political aristocracy while the citizenry has been indentured by rising public and private debt into debt-serfdom.

Let's now tie this back to our starting point from Part One: the purpose of education is to prepare students to establish and maintain a productive livelihood.

Though entrenched interests within the educational complex will naturally deny this, the current education system prepares students to serve failing neofeudal rentier arrangements, either as service workers or as technocratic managers. Though lip service is duly given to critical thinking, the education industry engenders social, political and economic conformity to a failed system.

The higher educational industry is itself a key part of this neofeudal arrangement. Indeed, its first order of business is to turn students into debt-serfs via state-guaranteed (and enforced) student loans. The education industry has morphed into another politically powerful cartel that produces and markets a standardized product, protected from real competition even as costs soar and the value of its output diminishes.

It not surprising that the education industry is incapable of exposing the failing institutions of the economy and social order, for it is one of the largest and most self-serving of these institutions. How can a cartel that has itself lost sight of its original mandate develop a critique of other cartels that wouldn't demystify its own collusion?

Before we start our overview of the emerging economy, it's important to remind ourselves that we are to some degree prisoners of our own era and experience. Beliefs drive actions, and experience shapes beliefs. We have difficulty imagining a different kind of economy and educational system because we naturally assume the current versions are the natural order of things. It seems to be human nature to assume present trends will extend linearly into the future, and that change will be marginal and well within the bounds of the current system. This belief in the present system as essentially eternal is akin to 1250 AD in Europe and Japan, when feudalism was the natural order of things. The idea that there could be some other structure to life did not exist.

Though the next iterations of capitalism and higher education are not yet entirely visible to us, we can discern the outlines of emerging alternatives: an increasingly decentralized, community-based economy coupled with a rising demographic of young people increasingly unwilling to indenture themselves to huge debts incurred by consumption and malinvestment, and a low-cost, highly adaptive form of higher education I term the Nearly Free University.

Chapter 5: The Dynamics of Economic Systems

What the global economy is experiencing not a crisis of capitalism or one political order—it is a crisis of the material and financial worlds: of resources, production, work, social stability and the distribution of surplus. It would still unfold even if money was sound, banks were well-regulated and politicians were not corrupt; it will unfold in monarchies, theocracies, socialist societies and capitalist economies with equal vigor.

Though the crisis will ultimately disrupt economies regardless of their ideological underpinnings or political system, capitalism plays a unique role in this process for two reasons: it is the dominant economic system, and as Marx understood, it is intrinsically disruptive and compelling by its very nature. In *The Communist Manifesto* (1848), Marx described the core dynamics of capitalism:

"The bourgeoisie has through its exploitation of the world market given a cosmopolitan character to production and consumption in every country. All old-established national industries have been destroyed or are daily being destroyed. They are dislodged by new industries, whose introduction becomes a life and death question for all civilized nations, by industries that no longer work up indigenous raw material, but raw material drawn from the remotest zones; industries whose products are consumed, not only at home, but in every quarter of the globe. In place of the old wants, satisfied by the production of the country, we find new wants, requiring for their satisfaction the products of distant lands and climes. In place of the old local and national seclusion and self-sufficiency, we have intercourse in every direction, universal inter-dependence of nations. And as in material, so also in intellectual production. The intellectual creations of individual nations become common property. National one-sidedness and narrow-mindedness become more and more impossible."

Author Jerry Muller (*The Mind and the Market: Capitalism in Western Thought*) has observed that capitalism's ceaseless creative destruction fuels insecurity and inequality even as it expands cultural possibilities and the means of self-cultivation, and extends the distribution not just of material commodities but of communication, information and entertainment—what might be called the appetites of the mind.

These benefits are compelling enough that individuals and societies around the globe have traded the stagnation of traditional forms of stability for the innovation and instability of capitalism when the choice becomes available.

Though we speak of socialism as an alternative economic system, virtually all nominally socialist or Communist nations rely on the surplus generated by their capitalist private sector to subsidize their state-owned enterprises and social spending. In practice, socialism is less a system of production than a system of redistribution of the wealth generated by capitalism.

As I hope I made clear in Chapters 3 & 4, Economic Darwinism and the internal dynamics of financialization, rising debt, diminishing returns and systemic misallocation of capital are undermining the current centralized, state-cartel version of global capitalism. This version has been successful for so long that most participants cannot imagine its failure or an alternative. But as we saw in the section on Economic Darwinism, this outsized success has rewarded concentrated financial engineering and risk at the expense of traits and policies that will be successful in the next iteration of capitalism: flexibility, distributed risk, relocalization, crowdsourced capital and self-organizing systems of production.

Just as no one in the early stage of the Industrial Revolution (1750-1800) could possibly foretell what would fall by the wayside and what would take its place in the transformation ahead, no one in the present can foretell precisely what will be destroyed or dislodged by the next iteration of capitalism. What we can predict is that those nations and communities that attract entrepreneurs and mobile capital in all its forms will prosper, for these are the factors Arrighi identified as key to capitalism's core drive, the accumulation of capital.

Supply and Demand

One dynamic that is present in all economies is supply and demand. In economies without open markets, supply and demand find expression in black markets and hoarding. If supply rises while demand remains stable, prices fall. If supply is stable but demand rises, prices rise. If supply declines while demand increases, prices skyrocket. If supply expands while demand falls, prices plummet. This dynamic is based not on an economic model but on basic human nature. In capitalism, this dynamic is supposed to be transparent, i.e. goods and services get exchanged in an open market that discovers price with every transaction.

The concept of supply and demand applies to virtually everything that can be exchanged: goods, services, labor, capital, credit, risk, insurance, hedging, financial securities, and even various types of currency (money). The indispensable elements of life fall into a special category that I call the FEW resources: food, energy and water. Demand may fluctuate for these essentials, but it will not fall to zero. There are substitutes within the broad categories of food and energy, but there is no substitute for some form of food, energy and water.

Mispricing Resources and Exploiting the Commons

Another intriguing feature of the supply and demand concept is what it cannot accurately price - as an example, the value of clean air, national parks or an uncorrupted government. There may be a generalized demand for these, but there is no exchange to price them. The difficulty in pricing these is intrinsic, for there are a number of unique dynamics that cannot be priced by conventional means, including external costs (the cost of pollution and its consequences that are not included in the price of goods) and the tragedy of the commons, a phrase coined by ecologist Garrett Hardin.

In his essay *The Tragedy of the Commons* (1968), Hardin describes what happens when the self-interest of each individual is served by exploiting the public commons for individual gain. When everyone sees the commons as free for the taking, the commons is soon destroyed for all. In other words, the benefits of exploiting the freely available community resources (air, water, grazing land, etc.) are outsized for the individual, but ultimately catastrophic for everyone when the common resources are destroyed by overuse or overuse.

Supply and demand discovering price is the natural result of open exchange; it is not unique to capitalism. Nor are external costs and the tragedy of the commons unique to capitalism; avarice and blindness to long-term consequences are attributes of human nature, not capitalism.

The Five Types of Capitalism

Broadly speaking, capitalism is an economic and social system based on private ownership and transparent markets for the exchange and distribution of goods and services. While these attributes of capitalism can be traced back to early trading communities, the modern version of capitalism depends on transparent markets not just for goods and services but also for capital, labor, risk and credit.

Transparent markets discover the price of goods, services, labor, capital, risk and credit, and as a result they provide discipline that discourages high-risk, low-return speculative bets, inefficiency and waste.

As noted earlier, some attributes of capitalism appear to be expressions of human nature rather than ideological constructs. The pursuit of self-interest drives competition and what Adam Smith called "the invisible hand" of the market. It is also the reason that capital seeks the highest return.

Self-interest all too easily veers into greed and avarice, and as a result all economic and political systems have the potential to exploit shared resources (i.e. the commons) and other people. Once Elites gather the power to harvest the system's surplus, they strive mightily to engineer the status quo to protect their power and perquisites. This is a feature not just of capitalism but of all social and political orders. The Elites in feudal societies, monarchies, theocracies and socialist systems all manage the system to preserve their power.

In my book *Resistance, Revolution, Liberation: A Model for Positive Change*, I outline the following five basic types of capitalism (though variations of these are equally visible in monarchies, theocracies and socialism):

1. Extractive

2. Exploitative

3. Enterprise

4. Marketing

5. Corporate/State

Extractive capitalism is based on the gain reaped by the extraction of an asset in the environment, such as a metals mine or fishery. Once the resource is depleted, capital moves on, seeking another high-yielding investment.

Exploitative capitalism is based on the monopolistic control of labor and other productive assets such as land. A classic example is a feudal estate or a plantation with indentured labor.

Enterprise capitalism rewards capital invested when the leverage of innovation and competitive advantage is greatest, and heaps the greatest gains on innovations in technology and other means of production.

Marketing capitalism is based on the stimulation of previously non-existent (and generally superfluous) wants and impulses. This generates, and profits from, the consumerist ideology—there is never enough of anything except insecurity and desire. Marketing capitalism requires ubiquitous access to credit as the fuel for instant gratification.

Corporate/State capitalism is the institutionalization of crony capitalism in partnership with the State: the State enables and protects quasi-monopolies to fund its own Elites and expenditures.

Most economies are a mix of all five types; what's important is which ones dominate the economy and the political machinery of the state.

Mobile Capital and Creative Destruction

One aspect of capitalism that disturbs many people is the mobile nature of capital—that capital will flow to the highest return, regardless of national borders or religious, national and ideological loyalties.

Capital that doesn't seek to expand will fall victim to capitalism's process of natural selection, what economist Joseph Schumpeter termed creative destruction: the only way innovation and productive investment can occur is if less productive investments and quasi-monopolies are dismantled and liquidated. As a result, corporations and those tasked with managing capital become (using Peter Drucker's invocation of an old Soviet phrase) rootless cosmopolitans, moving financial and human capital where they will earn the highest return. The same can be said of mobile workers, who move in order to find work or advance their career.

Just as financial capital must grow or face creative destruction, human capital—skills and knowledge—must also be constantly reworked to align with changing market and social forces.

From the long-term perspective of human development, extracting a living from Nature is inherently insecure. Hunter-gatherers have to constantly locate new (or renewed) sources of food and water, and agriculture without irrigation is exposed to the risks of drought, flood, insect infestations, etc. Traditional societies and economies were thus geared toward conserving the techniques and social systems that organized labor, authority, grain distribution, etc. in ways that reduced such insecurity. This desire for security favored traditional means of enforcing stability, but also discouraged risk and innovation.

Capitalist enterprises are organized solely to seek profit and expand capital, and as a result they disrupt established economies and societies. Since capitalism thrives on risk-taking, innovation, mobile capital and the free exchange of ideas, goods and services, it rewards disruptive improvements in productivity and new techniques of extraction, processing and manufacture. As a result, capitalism soon outpaces traditional methods, often by an order of ten (i.e. the new techniques and organizations produce ten times more than the equivalent traditional methods with the same input of labor).

Everything from the structure of families to the political order may be disrupted and changed by rapid changes in production and distribution of goods and services. As a result, there is always a tension between capitalism and the traditionally conservative social and political order.

It is important to understand the democratizing power of modern capitalism's financial system. The core features of modern finance— joint stock companies, stock exchanges and risk-management hedges— were present in European hotbeds of capitalism by the 1400s. Capitalism's ability to raise capital from diverse sources and lend it to a variety of enterprises enabled a new class—entrepreneurs—to arise. From that point on, enterprise was not limited to the aristocracy;

people outside the small circle of the Elite suddenly had access to capital.

Capitalism developed as an orderly way to share and price risk, and to spread losses from failed ventures and loans. By enabling small investors to pool capital, the system created a broad-based mechanism for distributing both profits and losses. In similar fashion, today the Internet is enabling crowdsourced, opt-in sources of credit such as micro-loans. Credit is escaping from the tyranny of the big banks and their partners, the central bank and state.

The Essential Role of Credit, Property Rights and Rule of Law

Property rights, rule of law and credit all have key roles in capitalism. Credit-starved economies with limited private ownership rights are underdeveloped economies, as economist Hernando De Soto explained in his book, *The Mystery of Capital: Why Capitalism Triumphs in the West and Fails Everywhere Else*. In the chronically underdeveloped economies De Soto describes, households have assets—land, dwellings, small businesses—but since the assets do not have legal status as "property" (because the system for recognizing and registering property is cumbersome and/or corrupt), the assets cannot act as collateral for borrowed capital (i.e. loans).

This highlights the essential role of the state in modern capitalism: a state must have the funding and legitimacy to establish, maintain and enforce a legal system that protects and regulates private property, open markets and credit.

A state that can be corrupted to protect and enrich entrenched Elites at the expense of the commons is a state where capitalism and democracy are stunted – and as a result, so too are opportunity and prosperity.

Credit plays a key role in capitalism's success and also its failure. When credit is unavailable to entrepreneurs, innovations go begging and the economy stagnates under entrenched Elites. Conversely, when credit is so cheap and plentiful that unproductive projects are funded, the eventual collapse of these malinvestments can bring down the entire financial system.

Colonial America provides an example of a credit-starved economy. In the wake of the Revolutionary war and the ratification of the Constitution (1789), the U.S. financial system was a mess: debts left by the war burdened the new government, which historian Thomas McCaw noted "started on a shoestring and almost immediately went bankrupt."

Ordinary farmers and entrepreneurs were desperate for long-term credit to fuel their rapidly growing enterprises. Though states were banned by the Constitution from issuing their own currency, states got around this prohibition by granting bank charters. The banks promptly issued the credit that an entrepreneurial economy needed. The political Elite, regardless of their differences, were appalled by this explosion of privately issued and largely unregulated credit, but this access to credit fueled the astonishing growth of the U.S. economy in the 1790's and early 1800's.

The nascent American economy in this phase was anything but orderly or well-regulated. The terms "wild" and "risky" better describe the financial and commercial chaos of the era, but this untamed capitalism led to more successes than failures. The chaotic explosion of credit and entrepreneurial drive was the opposite of central planning, be it Communist, theocratic or nominally capitalist. Risk was everywhere; security according to today's meaning did not exist.

Risk cannot be eliminated; it can only be suppressed or transferred to others. This is the lesson of mathematician Benoit Mandelbrot's book, *The Misbehavior of Markets: A Fractal View of Financial Turbulence*. Though government social welfare programs have eased the insecurity that comes with constant innovation and disruption, there is no way to eliminate risk from capitalism, or indeed, from life itself.

Cooperation, Innovation and Risk Management

One feature of capitalism that is rarely noted is the premium placed on cooperation. The Darwinian aspect of competition is widely accepted (and rued) as capitalism's dominant force, but cooperation is just as intrinsic to capitalism as competition. Subcontractors must cooperate to assemble a product, suppliers must cooperate to deliver the various components, distributors must cooperate to get the products to retail outlets, workers and managers must cooperate to pursue the goals of the organization, and local governments and communities must cooperate with enterprises to maintain the local economy.

Darwin's understanding of natural selection is often misapplied. In its basic form, natural selection simply means that the world changes constantly, and organisms must adapt or they will expire. The same is true of enterprises, governments, cultures and economies. Darwin wrote: "It is not the strongest of the species that survives, or the most intelligent, but the ones most adaptable to change." Ideas, techniques and processes which are better and more productive than previous versions will spread quickly; those who refuse to adapt them will be overtaken by those who do. These new ideas, techniques and processes trigger changes in society and the economy that are often difficult to predict.

This creates a dilemma: we want more prosperity and wider opportunities for self-cultivation, yet we don't want our security and culture to change in disruptive ways. But we cannot have it both ways. Ironically, those who attempt to preserve their power over the social order while reaping the gains of capitalism find their power dissolving before their eyes as unintended consequences of technological and social innovations disrupt their mechanisms of control.

Yet rejecting capitalism also fails to preserve the power structure, for a citizenry denied the opportunity to prosper chafes under a Status Quo that empowers Elites and relegates the masses to stagnation and poverty.

The great irony of capitalism is that the only way to establish an enduring security is to embrace innovation and adaptation, the very processes that generate short-term insecurity. Attempting to guarantee security leads to risk being distributed to others, or concentrated within the system itself. When the accumulated risk manifests, the system collapses.

The core dynamic of capitalism is the causal links between the free movement of labor and capital, transparent markets, risk, adaptation and growth. Every attempt to eliminate risk, hinder the flow of capital, rig markets and limit disruptive adaptation leads to stagnation and eventual collapse as the inefficient, wasteful and corrupt elements of the economy absorb all surplus from the system, starving the system of investment, innovation, accountability and initiative.

The Seventh Type of Capital: Community Capital

We touched on six types of capital in Chapter 2: financial, human, social, cultural, symbolic and infrastructure. There is one additional form of capital that I term community capital which is best understood by asking: what is indispensable in the practice of capitalism?

The standard answer is capital (money to invest in an enterprise) and labor (to operate the enterprise). However, if you drop a group of people (the labor) in the middle of a jungle with a bundle of cash (capital), you soon realize there are a number of other things that are indispensable to the practice of capitalism, including (1) institutions that facilitate cultural and symbolic capital and infrastructure (this harkens back to De Soto's insights into why capitalism works in the West and fails everywhere else: it requires institutions to record and enforce property rights and account for the money in bank accounts, loans and securities); (2) some widely distributed and trustworthy form of money—coins, letters of credit, paper currency, etc.—to facilitate the exchange of goods and services.; and (3) roads and waterways to facilitate moving goods to markets, and secure overseas trading routes to move goods to and from distant lands.

Infrastructure capital can be divided into large-scale networks of transport, communication and capital and localized social and material infrastructure. But capitalism does not just require human, social, cultural and symbolic capital and large-scale infrastructure—it also needs a fine-grained, small-scale, localized network of social and material capital: community capital. In the early capitalism described by Braudel, trading fairs and cities provided localized networks of markets, traders, suppliers and labor that acted as community capital.

In our era, Silicon Valley offers a well-known example of community capital. Geographically, it is a relatively small area, and though it has numerous financial and enterprise ties to the global economy, it remains a local community with a specific set of values, institutions and infrastructure. Personal connections still matter; so does trust. Running fast Internet connections and building office parks near universities does not recreate Silicon Valley, though that is a rough approximation of the physical infrastructure.

Community capital includes financial capital, human and social capital, local institutions and infrastructure but also a set of values and self-organizing networks of communication and trust. Locales with abundant community capital will be able to generate innovations and wealth out of proportion to their population or financial capital.

Human Capital, Social Capital, and Social Innovation

We discussed human capital and social capital in some detail in Chapter 2, but let's integrate these concepts into our understanding of labor and capitalism.

Social Capital

If you arrive in a strange city where you know no one, you have no social capital. You may have a map or guide and applicable travel experience, but with no contacts you have no social capital. Social capital is the sum of friends, contacts, alliances, memberships and networks that create reciprocal sources of value. Social capital is a two-way dynamic: it isn't created by decree but rather by providing value to others. Reciprocity is the heart of social capital.

Human Capital

Human capital is not the same as labor, because labor is interchangeable; human capital is not. As an example, consider a simple repetitive task in a factory or field. We can train someone to grab a part and bolt it to a chassis on an assembly line in a few moments. One person may be initially faster or slower at the task, but anyone with normal dexterity and mental faculties will be able to perform the task with very limited training. However, if a task requires a worker who cannot be replaced by someone taken off the street, that task requires human capital: knowledge, experience and skills.

The longer it takes to train someone to perform a task, the higher the level of human capital. The more experience it takes to master a task, the higher the level of human capital. The greater the number of skills needed to complete a task, the higher the level of human capital.

Human capital is difficult to narrowly define because it includes both values and soft skills, such as the ability to learn quickly (known in tech circles as having a high-bandwidth). Being able to communicate effectively is human capital; so is emotional intelligence. Being able to transfer skills from one job to another is a form of human capital.

Human capital is everything that is needed to complete tasks that cannot be taught in a few minutes. The more skills, knowledge and experience one possesses, the more human capital one has to leverage. The higher one's skill level, the higher the capital's value and potential income.

The Importance of Having Both Human and Social Capital

Neural networks are models of human capital: a communication can be exchanged very quickly when various nodes or people are connected to one another, as opposed to a linear chain of command. This network intelligence is the foundation of open-source enterprises, opt-in networks, and self-organizing systems, which evolve by following a set of opt-in rules rather than by following orders issued by a centralized bureaucracy.

The value in human networks is that the person you know might not be able to help you, but someone else they know might. The more people who know what you're seeking and what you have to offer, the more likely you'll be to meet someone who can help you. Trust is authenticated not by a centralized bureaucracy but by those who can vouch for your work and trustworthiness. The broad base of participants is the source of verification, not bureaucratic gatekeepers. The more people who have come to trust you to perform honestly and honorably as promised, the more opportunities will come your way. The more links of reciprocity you build, the broader your base of potentially helpful contacts.

Human groups are built on reciprocity and trust; that is the essence of social capital. The mover and shaker reached that level of influence not because he or she asked for a personal favor from everyone they met; they reached a position of influence by offering help and following through as promised.

Social capital has atrophied in many layers of our economy and culture. It is tempting to substitute a social-media contact for a personal connection. The social media contact may be useful, but is not a replacement for personal bonds of experience and trust.

Studies have found that human creativity is largely the result of sharing ideas and transferring innovations in one field to other fields. Innovation may arise from a single person, but its application requires human and social capital.

The two small-scale examples described below illustrate how human and social capital works in conjunction with infrastructure, community and financial capital.

Example 1: Farming as currently practiced is overwhelmingly industrial, and few would see any application of knowledge to the sector as being useful except to further the mechanization/automation of agribusiness. Yet highly educated people are profitably truck farming by applying their knowledge of marketing, food preparation and the restaurant business. For example, the trend-setting restaurant Chez Panisse in Berkeley, Calif., has a supply network of small farms, which in some cases are run by former employees of the restaurant. These small farmers are paid a good price for supplying very fresh organic produce. What is delivered daily sets the restaurant's menu for that day's lunch and dinner.

The key value creation in this arrangement is trust (social capital), attention to quality, and the ability to fashion menus around a variety of seasonal produce and meats (human capital). The labor of raising the produce is essential but it alone doesn't create the value.

Example 2: Street-Level Cycles in Berkeley, Calif., is an organization that partners long-abandoned city property with private enterprise to offer classes in bicycle repair and free use of the shop's tools to do-it-yourself types who want to repair their own bikes. It also provides bike repair services and sells used bicycles. The income generated by the repair service and sales of used bikes supports a small staff and enables the free community use of the shop's tools.

The amount of financial capital needed to start this enterprise was modest. The city-owned building was unoccupied for years. In exchange for use of the property, the city gets a self-funding, free community educational resource and service. The enterprise serves a wide spectrum of the community: students, do-it-yourselfers, those needing bike repairs or an inexpensive used bicycle. In offering the free classes to students, the enterprise has no competitors. In selling repair services and used bikes, it competes with other local bike shops. If someone wants to learn how to repair bicycles, this organization offers a nexus of tools and opportunities to learn and practice.

This low-cost synergy of local government, private enterprise, education, community service and social and human capital did not require any technological innovation—it required social innovation. It illustrates that the profit motive—often held up as the only motivator within capitalism—is not the only motivation for either innovation or enterprise.

These small-scale examples illustrate that innovation often takes what already exists in terms of financial and infrastructure capital and combines these ideas and resources into new methods of value creation. They also show that the key role of human and social capital in creating value via social innovation does not necessarily require more financial or infrastructure capital—and indeed may require less. This can be summarized as doing more with less.

Transformation arises from many sources, not just the technological innovations that receive media coverage. If we combine the many sources of transformation unleashed by digital technologies, we realize that ours is one of the great transformative eras in human history.

Values as the Incubator of Human and Social Capital

Our higher education system is based on the conviction that the primary impediment to universal prosperity is a lack of knowledge, which can be remedied with more education. This conviction cuts across ideological lines, as virtually everyone declares their belief in the economic value of education.

Since the key to prosperity is increasing productivity, the question becomes: does increasing a person's knowledge make them more productive? In some cases, the answer is clearly yes, but in other cases the answer is just as clearly no. Though it is politically sensitive, the difference between these two is based on the individual's value system and habits of behavior and thought. The key traits needed not just to learn effectively but to apply the knowledge productively are self-discipline and the abilities to focus for long periods of time, set aside current gratification for longer-term goals, persevere through difficulty and failure, work with others, and accept responsibility and remain accountable at all times, along with a desire to pursue interests and achieve mastery in the skills required to pursue those interests. All of this requires some self-knowledge and self-confidence as well as a cultural premium on education and mastery.

This ecosystem of values is established early in life within the family and community. It is not unique to any one culture, society or faith; it is universal and accessible to all. Becoming a productive person is not limited to any one sector of the economy, or any one level of native intelligence. Though these values and habits are first acquired (or not acquired) in the family and community, they can be acquired later in life if the student is willing to learn.

A large body of research supports this intuitively sensible connection between the values acquired in the home and future productivity and prosperity. For example, the quantity and variety of books in the household is a better predictor of students' test scores than household income. Though wealthier families have the financial resources to offer their children more enrichment (after-school classes, for example), the immigrant experience in America provides countless examples of families arriving with no financial assets who manage by dint of unceasing effort and thrift to lift their children into the prosperous class of highly educated and productive citizens.

Conventional education assumes these values will be absorbed by osmosis or occasional lip service offered within standard coursework; unfortunately there is little evidence for this osmosis theory, and plenty of evidence that the gap between those with these values and those lacking these values widens in a factory-model school rather than narrows. Economists Pedro Carneiro and James Heckman concluded: "Differences in cognitive and noncognitive skills by family income and family background emerge early and persist. If anything, schooling widens these early differences."

In other words, conventional education benefits those who already possess the values and qualities that make them educable.

There are several factors in these differences. Educated parents clearly value education, as their own behavior exhibits the commitment and values needed to pursue higher education. Emotionally nurturing parents and caregivers instill the self-confidence needed to persevere through failure and criticism, and a culturally nurturing family provides the intellectual stimulation and human capital of early exposure to music, religion, the arts, positive ethnic identity and exposure to the social capital of cultural institutions.

As Jerry Muller wrote in a recent essay on *Capitalism and Inequality*, "Each generation of social scientists discovers anew (and much to their chagrin), the resources transmitted by the family tend to be highly determinative of success in school and the workplace."

There is little mystery about what separates highly accomplished, successful and prosperous families from those who struggle financially. The accomplished families are invariably led by parents who lead by example. Parents who play a musical instrument for pleasure reveal the payoff for the hard work of learning to play music, and those who serve on church or community committees illustrate the satisfaction and benefits of serving others. Parents who pursue interests and improve their own mastery outside of school or the workplace pass these values on to their children.

Additionally, though one would not know it from mainstream media coverage, financial wealth is still linked causally to the values of thrift and productive use of capital. Remarkably, developing human and social capital does not necessarily require wealth or high income. Rather, a key determinant of human capital (psychological resilience, self-confidence and emotional intelligence) is the amount of nurturing time parents spend with their children and the parents' expectations of their children behavior and values.

Mainstream financial and social success depends on networks and connections—social capital that is enabled by human capital. Those with more human capital are better able to take advantage of opportunities to build social capital than those with minimal human capital. Many feel that the real advantage of attending an elite university is not the quality of the instruction per se but the opportunities to form friendships and professional connections that open doors unavailable to those outside the institutions. In other words, it is the social capital that counts, not the knowledge gained.

However, it requires an abundance of human capital to exploit these opportunities: the social skills of knowing how to dress and interact with accomplished people, knowing how to present (but not oversell) oneself, possessing the broad cultural knowledge necessary to understand the terms and contexts of conversations and situations, the self-confidence and humility needed to be a beginner, being a good listener, being able to recruit a mentor, and so on.

Little of this human capital is related to one's educational level or classroom knowledge. If creativity is causally linked to the networking of creative people and new ideas, then one's network is more of a determinant of success than educational attainment per se – and research supports this contention. The goal of human and social capital is to develop what I term network intelligence: the creativity and connections that arise from participating in productive networks. The upper-class family is wealthy not just in assets, but in social capital, connections that open doors or solve problems in ways that are unavailable to the less well-connected.

If the family and perhaps our genetic heritage establish our basic human and social capital, then what role does education play, other than widening the existing gaps? It is my contention that education can only increase productivity and the acquisition of human and social capital in two ways: (1) helping students learn how to learn, making the student the teacher; and (2) explicitly teaching the values, behaviors and habits that are needed to build human and social capital.

Causes of Inequality

There are three basic causes of economic inequality:

1. The dynamic nature of capitalism, which rewards innovations that increase productivity;

2. Financialization and the resultant political corruption, which favor the wealthy with access to credit and political influence; and

3. Differences in values and human and social capital, which lead to equivalent differences in productivity and prosperity.

Despite decades of focusing on education as the panacea for inequality, the failure of conventional education (the transmission of knowledge) to reduce inequality is now understandable, as conventional education does not address any of these causes.

Capitalism rewards competition, cooperation, capital accumulation, innovation, adaptability and risk-taking when these boost productivity. Those who are unable or unwilling to improve their productivity will fall behind, unless they are wealthy enough to have the state create a subsidy, cartel or quasi-monopoly that enriches them.

The gross inefficiencies and distortions of financialization will collapse the financial sector and the state, but until that collapse occurs the political capture of the state by financial Elites makes reform essentially impossible. Instead of bemoaning this inevitable collapse, we can prepare ourselves for the emerging economy that is not dependent on financialization or state-cartel crony capitalism for its vigor or prosperity.

In order to accomplish this, the education industry must be re-oriented to the two basic goals listed above:

1. Helping students learn how to learn, making the student the teacher

2. Explicitly teaching the values, behaviors and habits needed to build human and social capital.

This is an old story, of course: give a man a fish and you feed him for a day; teach him how to fish and he will feed himself for a lifetime. The point of this section is to describe the complexity of becoming productive; it is not a matter of providing or absorbing knowledge; instead it requires an understanding of the essential role of values and human and social capital.

Those lacking the necessary values can learn how to acquire them. With those values, behaviors and habits in hand, acquiring knowledge, human and social capital becomes not just possible but inevitable.

Value and the Tyranny of Price

As discussed earlier, clean air, national parks and an uncorrupted government are examples of resources for which the value cannot be priced. Superficially, the price of a good or service is presumed to express all costs and value, but this assumption is false. The external costs of a product, for example the cost of disposing of the product or the environmental cleanup required a decade hence from its manufacture, are not in the retail price and indeed cannot be accurately determined because the costs are in the future.

Transparent markets do not just discover price; they also enable the valuation of intangibles. Price is only one function of value.

Global corporations worship price because that is the primary advantage they extract from their economies scale and global supply chains. We are constantly instructed by corporate marketing that the sole criterion of value is price—what my colleague Bart Dessart calls crazy low prices.

Consider a loaf of bread. Corporate marketing would have us believe that price is the sole arbiter of value: the lowest priced loaf of bread is the best value. This reductionist definition of value excludes the nutritive content, the taste, the texture, and the pleasure of eating the bread from the valuation process. It also excludes the external costs that society eventually pays when people consume low-quality food. Given that healthcare now consumes almost 20% of the $16 trillion U.S. economy, these costs are non-trivial.

A loaf of locally produced artisan bakery bread has a higher price than the factory loaf, but the value is not in price alone. The local bakery bread cannot be valued by price alone, for it is not only enjoyable to eat (unlike the soft, tasteless factory bread) but with locally produced cheese or meat it becomes part of a memorable meal.

How do we currently value those tangible and intangible qualities? We calculate the true value and pay the modestly higher price for a much higher value product and experience.

A poorly made product has a low price but this doesn't necessarily reflect the lifetime value compared to a higher quality, higher priced product. If a poor-quality hand sander fails after a few months while a higher-quality sander that costs 50% more lasts ten times longer, the crazy low priced product is a poor value, despite its low price.

Results and process both generate valuations. If a global corporation manufactures a product with essentially slave labor, the corporation naturally attempts to focus our attention on the results, the crazy low prices, rather than the process that generated the results, the exploitation of impoverished workers.

As consumers in a marketplace, we are free to value process, not just results. Corporations loathe and fear a valuation of process, of course, unless they have a process that adds value to their product. This brings us to the tyranny of price, the ceaseless marketing of price as the sole criterion of value. If the processes and products are indeed identical, then price may be the primary differentiation other than brand (which adds or subtracts value as a signifier of status).

But in the localized community economy, we may frequent a restaurant, for example, that must charge higher prices than a global fast-food corporation because it lacks the corporation's economies of scale, access to cheap capital and politically-driven subsidies and tax shelters. We can choose to pay a modestly higher price because we receive much greater value by supporting people who live and work in our local community.

The emerging localized economy enables a much more transparent market for assessing value outside of the tyranny of price, which naturally favors corporations and cartels that source materials and labor globally and purchase subsidies and tax shelters from the state.

Financial and Project Management Skills

The process of creating value requires a systemic method of assessing and measuring that value. This includes price and profit but is not limited to these, as we have seen the intrinsic limits to relying on price to reflect value. This is the basis for the eighth essential skill, a practical working knowledge of financial and project management.

The dynamics of capitalism require a metric for measuring and tracking financial capital (labor, credit and cash) and accounting for risk and projected yield. These are the core tasks of financial management.

Managing human and social capital and intelligent networks is the core task of project management.

Both types of management skills will be required in the new economy.

Summary

Capitalism is a dynamic, self-organizing system that constantly evolves to lower risk and increase yield by shifting resources, labor, credit and capital in a matrix of cooperation and competition. Though conventional descriptions focus on the marketplace of price, supply and demand, we have seen that a specific set of values is essential to the actual practice of creating human/social capital and value, and that price alone does not reflect value in all circumstances.

If we combine the demise of the debt-based state-cartel Capitalism described in previous chapters with the intrinsically disruptive dynamics described in Chapters 3 & 4, we understand that the disintegration of the state-cartel status quo is actually an expression of capitalism's core dynamics. Diminishing returns inevitably lead to the creative destruction of phantom collateral as well as the political and social systems that were based on that collateral.

In terms of preparing students for the emerging economy, we now understand the essential role of values and intelligent networks in assembling the human and social capital needed to create value, and the need for students to learn how to assess and track the complex interaction of value and price.

Chapter 6: An Outline of the Emerging Economy

All economies and societies are battlegrounds between the status quo that benefits from the current distribution of power and wealth and the forces of innovation that could fatally disrupt the status quo. In eras of broadly rising productivity, this battle results in low-intensity volatility on the margins of the economy. We experience these fluctuations as cycles of rising and declining credit, productivity and profit, i.e. cycles of growth and recession.

But in eras of systemic fragility resulting from rising debts and diminishing returns, this conflict triggers an endgame: either the status quo successfully suppresses innovation, in which case the economy stagnates, or the forces of innovation fatally destabilize the status quo. Either way, the result is the same: the system enters a crisis and is fundamentally transformed.

Those in power hope to adopt only those aspects of innovation they can harness to increase their own wealth and power, but the forces of innovation cannot be tamed, gamed or distributed according to political favoritism. Innovation inevitably leaps across the status quo's moats and disrupts the old order.

Since capitalism is intrinsically disruptive, the cartels and the state that protects them must suppress the four key dynamics of capitalist disruption: competition, innovation, transparency and the creative destruction of unproductive arrangements and assets.

The state is by definition a monopoly, so it is free from competition and can actively suppress any threats posed by innovation or transparency. As the state's power has expanded, it has protected itself from creative destruction; the state is free to impose unproductive subsidies on the economy until the economy implodes, bringing the state down with it.

Cartels are by definition anti-competitive; their most profitable arrangement is not open competition but monopoly and price-fixing. Cartels only accept those innovations which benefit their profit margins, and they actively resist creative destruction of their state subsidies.

When innovations serve the interests of cartels, the economy registers growth as the cartels adopt the improved technology and productivity increases. The global economy of the 1950's and 1960's offers an example of this dynamic. However, when innovations dry up or threaten the status quo, the economy stagnates as input costs rise and productivity lags, as in the 1970's.

Stimulus by the state (monetary and fiscal policy) fails to reignite productivity and growth, as the systemic problem can only be solved by creative destruction of what is no longer productive, and this includes state subsidies and central bank policies. The stagflation of the 1970s, for example, only ended when easy-money Federal policies ceased and American industry restructured.

It is no accident that disruptive technologies—for example, the Internet and personal computers—have only emerged in sectors that are neither controlled by the state nor dominated by an existing cartel.

When these technologies do not directly threaten the status quo's power and wealth, they are free to expand. But the sectors that are still reaping productivity gains are simply too small to support an economy burdened by an inefficient state and its protected cartels.

Freed of the discipline of competition and protected from creative destruction, state institutions (fiefdoms) and cartels (military-industrial complex, education industry, healthcare, finance, mortgages, etc.) become increasingly costly to maintain even as the value of their output diminishes. (Examples include the $1 trillion F-35 Lightning program for a fighter that costs four times as much as the F-18 Hornet it replaces and healthcare, which has expanded to almost 20% of the economy while overall health stagnates or declines.)

As a result, the cost of maintaining these inefficiencies absorbs an increasing share of the national surplus. In effect, supporting these inefficient sectors acts as an enormous tax on the productive sectors. Protecting inefficient sectors introduces moral hazard and imposes opportunity costs: a productive investment must be sacrificed to subsidize unproductive protected sectors.

As outlined in Chapter 3, this forces the state into an impossible quandary: the only way the state can meet its dual obligations (supporting the cartels and increasing social spending) is to borrow vast sums of money, creating another quandary: the debt must be eventually renounced or inflated away, or the rising interest will erode the state's ability to fund its obligations.

If innovation and creative destruction are not allowed to restructure the state and its cartels, these inefficient sectors eventually collapse under their own weight. As noted above, the productive sectors of the economy cannot support ever-expanding trillion-dollar inefficiencies and deficits.

Managers within the state and cartels have no incentive to risk adopting innovation that could disrupt the organization, and every incentive to suppress such threats. These risk calculations only change at the point where doing nothing will lead to collapse. Only then will managers be willing to risk structural innovations. At that point, the inefficiencies and unproductive culture are so ingrained that the organization cannot be salvaged.

These dynamics leave the innovative sectors little room within the conventional state-cartel economy. As a result, the emerging economy is largely arising outside the state-cartel debtocracy. The forces of transformation will only be free to creatively destroy inefficient and unproductive subsidies within the state and its favored cartels when the barriers erected by the state become too costly to maintain. When the state's barriers crumble, then all sectors of the economy will be exposed to competition and creative destruction, including the state itself.

A competitive economy reduces costs and creatively destroys sectors that were skimming profits from state-enforced rentier arrangements. Lowering costs requires reducing labor's share, which reduces payroll taxes collected by the state. Competition leads to lower profits, which further reduces state tax revenues. Competition necessarily leads to a smaller, leaner state.

As noted previously, capitalism is not just an economically disruptive force; it is equally disruptive of social and political structures that have been constructed on the unstable ground of debt, phantom collateral and diminishing returns.

We naturally decry the loss of our own monopoly/rentier arrangement, along with the social and political security that arrangement enabled. But when monopoly/rentier arrangements come to dominate the economy, the increasing costs and diminishing yields lead to collapse. This is happening to national economies across the globe, regardless of their ideology or political order.

Every economy faces the same quandary: retaining cartels and rentier arrangements will bring down the state and the economy, but enabling competition will creatively destroy monopolies and rentier arrangements, leading to a much smaller, leaner state. Either way, the economy is disrupted and the state is reduced.

The choice is simple: support the debt-based consumerist economy and the state-cartel status quo and experience its inevitable collapse, or accept the insecurity and disruption that arises from innovation, transparency and competition.

Ours Is a Transformational Era

The conventional view of our economy is that the current stagnation is merely a cyclical "rough patch" that can be cured with additional debt-based spending on pretty much anything and everything: Bridges to Nowhere, fighter jets that cost four times more while being less capable than the planes they replace, $1 trillion in student loans for marginal-utility college degrees, and a healthcare system that spends twice as much per person as competing economies but yields declining national health.

As I have explained in Chapters 3, 4 & 5, this is not a "rough patch" in a conventional business cycle; deeply structural trends have ripened into an endgame where every path leads to the same conclusion: the end of an increasingly fragile, unsustainable status quo.

Those without an understanding of the systemic forces at work confuse cycles with trends. As I have repeatedly noted, those living in transformational eras cannot imagine the next era, as they naturally assume the current era is permanent and every crisis is cyclical, i.e. temporary. Few residents of Imperial China in 1639, for example, foresaw that in a mere five years the mighty Ming Empire would collapse in a heap. Beneath the reassuring veneer of permanence, the

Empire's systemic fragility left it increasingly vulnerable to financial crises.

We are in a similar era today. We can discern systemic fragility and vulnerability, but the timing and nature of the transformation ahead is unknowable.

Though no one can know the future, we can identify the sources of systemic fragility and stability. If we cling to policies that increase systemic fragility and suppress the sources of systemic stability, the transformation will be messy and destructive. If we abandon all that increases systemic fragility and invest in sources of systemic stability and vitality, the transformation will be messy but creative.

The Systemic Source of Stability and Security

State-cartel monopoly/rentier arrangements create financial security for those within the fiefdom's moat, but they do so by sacrificing the long-term systemic stability offered by competition, transparency and innovation. Eventually, the inexorable increase in input costs and the diminishing yield of these arrangements cause them to implode. The security they offer is thus temporary.

Ironically, long-term security depends on rising productivity and productive investment of all forms of capital. This long-term security requires accepting the permanent low-intensity volatility of creative destruction, innovation and competition.

This is the context of the emerging economy, what could be termed Capitalism 2.0.

The Limits of the State and Market Sectors

If we had to identify the one critical structural cause of the endgame, it would be the limits of the state and market sectors of the economy. The market economy generates a wealth of goods and services as owners, managers and investors pursue profits and capital. The forces of competition and new labor-saving technologies have made profits and capital accumulation largely dependent on reducing labor. The market economy no longer has need for the workforce. As a result, wages are no longer an adequate model for distributing the surplus generated by the economy.

The state's social-welfare solution to this structural decline of paid work is to redistribute surplus by collecting taxes to fund more social spending. In effect, the state's solution is to tax the productive and pay those without jobs to be unproductive. For all the reasons outlined in previous chapters, the productive sectors face diminishing profits. As a consequence, the state must borrow immense sums of money to subsidize its inefficient fiefdoms and cartels and fund higher social spending. This reliance on debt is self-liquidating, i.e. eventually the debt limits the state's ability to borrow more and the debt-dependent system collapses.

The state does not create surplus; it takes a slice of the surplus generated by the private market economy. As the surplus shrinks, the state's share must also shrink, or taxes must increase. At some point, higher taxes starve the private market economy of capital and its ability to generate surplus rapidly declines, creating a self-reinforcing feedback loop of higher taxes and state spending and declining surpluses that can be taxed.

In other words, the decline of paid work cannot be fixed by either the market or state sectors. The solutions must arise within the atrophied and largely underdeveloped community sector of the economy.

Transformation Only Occurs When There Is No Other Option

It is human nature to conserve what seems to be working well enough and reject any change that might threaten our security and share of the status quo. Transformation is simply not worth the risk when things are working tolerably well. As a result, we only embrace intrinsically risky systemic change when there is no other choice, i.e. the current status quo is collapsing around us and all attempts to conserve it have failed.

As long as the current debt-based consumerist state-cartel system remains in place, the vast majority of participants have little incentive to invest time and resources in alternatives.

Increasingly fragile systems tend to appear stable right up the point they collapse. We can anticipate this will be the case with our consumerist state-cartel debtocracy: it will appear secure and enduring right up the moment it crumbles.

At that point, everyone will be seeking models and templates that can generate some semblance of the stability and security lost in the demise of the old order. The key characteristics of the emerging economy help us identify models and templates that offer systemic stability and security in the era ahead.

Key Characteristics of the Emerging Economy (Capitalism 2.0)

Examples of the emerging economy are currently visible in many sectors. In finance, crowdsourced funding is offering an alternative to the conventional investment-banking cartel. In healthcare, cash-only services and medical tourism are expanding outside the insurance-Medicare cartels. In the defense industry, new drone manufacturers have arisen outside the military-industrial cartel. Free college-level courses from organizations like the Khan Academy and Saylor.org are emerging as forces outside the education cartel.

Innovation is not limited to technology; it can also be social. The local farmers' markets that are providing alternatives to agribusiness, for example, are not technological innovations, though new Web technologies are aiding their expansion. The explosive rise in car-sharing is also a social innovation, as the younger generation accepts the concept of access not ownership (which can be described as the systemic reappraisal of the opportunity cost of ownership).

Though the emerging economy favors faster, better, cheaper, it also makes room for those who value process in addition to price. In other words, there is a spectrum of valuation in the emerging economy, as opposed to the monoculture of crazy low prices being the sole arbiter of value.

The emerging economy has a handful of key characteristics:

1. Emerging-economy enterprises do not replace the existing state-corporate economy—they broaden the spectrum of opportunities and choices. Worker-owned cooperatives such as the Cheese Board in Berkeley, California don't replace conventional corporate supermarkets, any more than car-share companies like ZipCar replace corporate car-rental companies. Crowd-funding sites like KickStarter don't replace too big to fail banks, they widen the spectrum of possibilities for small businesses to find funding.

The Co-op Academy in New York City offers a curriculum and opportunity that is not available at conventional four-year universities: hands-on training in starting and operating a cooperative enterprise.

In some cases, emerging-economy enterprises compete with established businesses by offering a new model—for example, Airbnb offers private rooms and flats as an alternative to hotels. New web-enabled, decentralized models and services offer competitive advantages in price and quality, often by broadening the range of prices and services offered.

2. The emerging economy offers alternative infrastructures and models that do not depend on direct state or corporate funding or participation. These alternative infrastructures are often self-organizing networks that organize and distribute work, risk, profit, technology and ideas through non-state, non-corporate distribution channels.

For example, consider project management. Within the state or global corporation, every aspect of the project from management to funding must filter through a complex bureaucratic hierarchy. The emerging economy/Capitalism 2.0 model is to assemble a working group (that might be sourced locally or globally, depending on the project) to complete the work with minimal layers of oversight. Once the project is completed, the group disperses and its members move on to other jobs. This model favors flexibility, frugality and productive use of capital and resources.

In this model, careers in the emerging economy are adaptive ecosystems of collaboration and work.

3. These alternative infrastructures empower and broaden the community economy, the localized economy that has largely been superseded by the state and corporate sectors in the current state-cartel system.

One example of such an alternative infrastructure is the "labor bank." Participants voluntarily join the bank and contribute hours of labor to help other members or community projects. Hours that have been "banked" can be traded for other members' services. No money changes hands in these transactions, and so the exchange is entirely outside the state and corporate sectors.

4. The transformative power of these non-state, non-corporate models lies in their scalability and adaptability, i.e. they can be freely copied, adapted to local conditions and expanded. Many non-state, non-corporate models have long histories, for example, cooperatives, worker-owned enterprises, and community land banks. The emerging economy has enabled the sharing and adaption of these models and introduced new ones that have been enabled by the Internet and Web-based technologies—for example, the "labor bank."

5. Emerging-economy technologies (digital-software-fabrication-robotics-automation—DSFRA) are transforming state and corporate organizations as budget pressures force agencies and institutions to cut costs. One example is the reduction of the crew on trash collection trucks from three (one driver and two people to pick up the trash bins) to one, as a mechanical arm operated by the driver picks up and empties the bins. This example shows that even traditional services such as trash collection are not impervious to radical reductions in costs once budget constraints force agencies to explore emerging-economy innovations.

6. The emerging economy's potential for web-enabled processes to transform state and corporate functions has yet to be explored, much less implemented. Decentralized, transparent, opt-in ways of fulfilling state responsibilities have yet to be fully imagined.

    Consider the process of local governments' reviewing blueprints and issuing building permits—a typically centralized and time-consuming process. One emerging-economy solution to lower costs and dramatically speed up the process would be to accredit plan checkers and then establish a competitive queue online that matched up citizens seeking building permits with plan checkers. A plan checker with no current project might offer to process a set of blueprints for less than colleagues who had a backlog of other projects. Planners guaranteeing a fast turn-around could charge a premium if customers were willing to pay more for faster service.

Planners who failed to deliver as promised would receive negative reviews online until they improved their service.

This model of matching customers and processors in competitive, transparent queues could be applied to a variety of state services.

7. No one knows which models and ideas will be most productive in a particular enterprise or community, and so the emerging economy embraces experimentation, trial-and-error and sharing of what worked and what didn't, and why. Top-down solutions issued by centralized authorities might not work across a multiplicity of situations, and an evolving mix of solutions might work best.

   How is this different from the market economy? Not every problem can be solved in a way that generates a profit. This is the limit intrinsic to the market. How can safe bike lanes be a profitable business if the bike lanes are free? How can keeping the bike lanes cleared of trash be a profitable business if users don't pay to use the bike lanes? Clean, safe free bike lanes create tremendous value without being profit centers in the market economy.

   The market and state sectors of the economy have inherent limits; neither can solve all problems within their models of generating profits and raising taxes or loading staggering debts on future taxpayers.

8. Emerging-economy models and enterprises may compete with the state and corporate sectors in some cases and collaborate with them in others; in cases such as labor banks, they may operate outside the state and corporate sectors. There is no limitation on the range or scope of emerging-economy models, infrastructures and enterprises; the core principle is to create value and increase capital of all types by sharing and adapting the most productive model and technology.

9. The key traits of the emerging economy are flexibility and adaptability. The emerging economy embodies Darwin's observation that "It is not the strongest of the species that survives, or the most intelligent, but the ones most adaptable to change."

From Marginal to Mainstream

Many of these dynamics are still on the margins of the current state-cartel economy, and it is easy to dismiss them as outliers. But social and technological innovations alike can be adopted and go mainstream with remarkable rapidity. The Pareto distribution is a useful guide to this process. As an example, when only 2% of adult Americans were Internet users, the technology had little effect on the overall society and economy. But when 4% of adults became users, this had an outsized influence on 64% of the populace. Once 20% of adults obtained an Internet connection, within a few short years 80% were on the Internet.

The social and political upheaval of the 1960s spread quickly around the world in a few short years. This is typical of transformative eras.

We should be cautious about dismissing emerging trends as inconsequential, for they often follow the Pareto distribution of building momentum very gradually and then suddenly becoming influential once the trend hits critical mass. This dynamic mirrors Hemingway's famous response in *The Sun Also Rises* to the question, how did you go bankrupt? "Two ways," Mike said. "Gradually and then suddenly."

Systemizing Adaptability and Innovation

Becoming more adaptable is not something that can be learned in conventional coursework, yet along with the ability to teach oneself new skills and knowledge throughout one's life, it must be the core purpose of education aimed at preparing students for the emerging economy (i.e. Capitalism 2.0). These two are intimately related, of course; knowing how to learn new material and apply it effectively in the real world is the key trait of adaptability.

There are several other features of adaptability than can be learned. One is learning to apply new knowledge to another field. In his book *The Post-Capitalist Society*, Peter Drucker noted that major leaps often occur when new knowledge from one field is applied to an unrelated field, a process that is often called cross-pollination or interdisciplinary research. As noted previously, creativity is fostered when ideas and people are networked, sharing ideas and innovations across fields. Adaptability is thus intertwined with both lifelong learning and innovation.

In Drucker's view, organizations that wish to avoid creative destruction must institutionalize innovation: "Every organization will have to learn how to innovate—and to learn that innovation can and should be organized as a systemic process." The same can be said of individuals and households.

Drucker identified three basic types of innovation. The first type is systemic improvement of everything done—what the Japanese call Kaizen. The second is to exploit one's successes by applying them to new products and/or services, building value by applying successful approaches to new fields. The third is the creation of something completely new. Unless these three basic types of innovation are systemically carried out, Drucker warned, the organization will soon become obsolete.

As we have seen, the status quo tries to avoid the pressure to adapt and innovate by digging moats of monopoly and political influence. But this subsidy has a high opportunity cost, since capital and income that could have been invested productively is instead spent propping up the most corrupt and least efficient sectors of the economy. As the protected sectors increase their share of the economy, the productive sectors are starved of capital and expertise.

There are a number of analogies that apply to this choice between conserving an increasingly inefficient institution and systemizing adaptability and innovation. One is the difference between a dead, brittle branch and a supple living one: when the wind rises, the brittle branch snaps while the supple one bends. Adaptability is flexibility is resilience.

Another analogy can be found in forestry management. If small brush fires are suppressed, eventually the forest's deadwood piles higher and higher to the point that when a fire finally does start, there is no controlling the conflagration. Similarly, if creative destruction is suppressed within institutions, the deadwood of inefficiency, mission creep and self-aggrandizement pile up, increasing the organization's vulnerability to collapse.

As Charles Darwin understood, adaptability is the key to survival, not just of individuals but households, institutions, enterprises, nations and species.

Multiple Skills, One Person

Having multiple skills is an aspect of adaptability that is generally under-appreciated. Not only does possessing multiple skills open more opportunities for productive work, it also seeds creativity within the individual, as a variety of experiences and skills create an interdisciplinary network within the individual. Learning additional skills also improves our learning how to learn skills.

An economy of multi-skilled people who wear a number of different hats is an entrepreneurial economy with a built-in ability to adapt, innovate and expand. These traits characterize the early decades of the U.S., and they inform our understanding of the emerging economy.

Albert Gallatin, Secretary of the Treasury under presidents Jefferson and Madison, was keenly aware of the unique way Americans combined a variety of skills and enterprises in each individual. In a speech to the House of Representatives in 1799, Gallatin explained that the occupations in Britain "were so well distinguished that a merchant and a farmer rarely combined in the same person; a merchant is a merchant, and nothing but a merchant; a farmer is a farmer and nothing but a farmer; but this is not the case in this country." But in America, "the different professions are blended together in the same person, the same man being frequently a farmer and a merchant and perhaps a manufacturer."

This is not just a cultural trait; it is the result of political and economic systems that enable freedom of movement and adaptability. Gallatin understood that America's development owed much of its success to "the absence of those systems of internal restrictions and monopoly which continue to disfigure the state of society in other nations."

This may seem at odds with the increased specialization that characterizes the modern economy, i.e. becoming more specialized to increase one's value in the marketplace. Those who combine multiple skills in one person serve different needs and dynamics, and even the specialist benefits from having a spectrum of skills to draw upon.

"Multiple skills, one person" supports what I term hybrid work and others term patchwork careers, the assembly of multiple sources of income that I describe later in this chapter. Another way of describing this is what my Australian colleague Bart Dessart calls *full-spectrum adaptability*, a spectrum of skills broad enough to enable the owner to adapt to any number of challenges and circumstances.

Developing multiple skills and networks builds ecosystems of collaboration and work in which security and stability arise not from state or corporate guarantees but from the systemic stability and vitality of these work-related ecosystems.

The DATA Model

If we had to summarize the key traits of the emerging economy listed above, I would choose the DATA model: decentralized, adaptable, transparent, and accountable, a model I described in my previous book, *Why Things Are Falling Apart and What We Can Do About It*. It is no coincidence that these are the opposite traits of the current state-cartel system, which is highly centralized, sclerotic, purposefully obscure and not accountable except to the Elites at the top of the pyramid. The important point here is that the current system's institutions cannot be decentralized, adaptable, transparent, and accountable, for they are the wrong unit size and the wrong organizational structure.

Peter Drucker noted that organizations in the emerging economy must be decentralized when he stated: "Its organizations must be able to make fast decisions, based on closeness to performance, closeness to the markets, closeness to technology, and closeness to changes in society, environment and demographics, all of which must be seen and utilized as opportunities for innovation."

In other words, adaptability requires decentralization.

Transparency is a threat to state-cartel organizations, as any exposure of internal dealings has the potential to disrupt the status quo. The lowest-risk way to manage a state-cartel organization is to hide all key agendas and actions and to purposefully obscure the facts to minimize resistance and cover up failures. The incentives within of centralized organization favor hiding anything that could be criticized by outside forces or that could disrupt the power of the organization itself.

Whatever cannot be completely hidden can be buried in lengthy reports or purposefully obscured with jargon and mind-numbing financial reports.

As an example of this, my local school district, which is responsible for the education of 9,800 students in kindergarten through grade 12, routinely issues a 230-page interim budget. This weighty document does not include any accounting of how many people are employed by the district or how much they are paid in salaries and benefits. In response to my inquiry, I was informed that no such accounting exists. I was told someone would "look into it," but I never received any response.

Without transparency, accountability has not just been lost; it is no longer even possible. This is the precise goal of those seeking to protect their pay, power and perquisites from exposure to inquiry.

This need for decentralization, adaptability, transparency and accountability pits the emerging economy against the interests of these established, centralized, sclerotic institutions. That the institution no longer serves its original purpose matters far less than maintaining the payroll of the institution, and doing so by any means necessary.

If a private firm with a large payroll goes bankrupt and closes its doors, community leaders bemoan the loss of jobs but soon revert to touting the empty facility as ideal for another enterprise. Conversely, if a military base, hospital or college closes down, the reaction is quite different; it's as if the very heart of the community has been ripped out and crushed by evil forces. In other words, these sacrosanct sectors of the economy, supported by one and all, can only expand; contraction is not allowed, even if the institution has lost its way and no longer serves its stated purpose.

As Drucker wrote: "For the school or the college to discharge its social function, we must be able to close down a school or college—no matter how deeply rooted in the local community and how much loved by it—if changes in demographics, technology, or knowledge make a different size or different philosophy a prerequisite of good performance."

In the emerging economy, if a community wants to keep its local institution free from any accountability, the community can specifically make the political decision to subsidize that institution with its own money, i.e. diverting income from some other purpose to pay the institution's costs. (As noted earlier, this creates moral hazard and raises the opportunity cost: what else cannot be funded so that this institution is free from accountability?)

This would soon focus attention on the institution's execution of its stated purpose and its efficiency, for when we have to directly pay for failure and waste, we become considerably less tolerant of the expense.

Managing Adaptation/Innovation

The emerging economy will require organizations of all sizes and types to systemize and manage adaptation and innovation. This in turn will require managers with the values and skills to manage change rather than manage with the goal of maintaining the Status Quo's pay, power and perquisites.

Once institutions are able to tap a permanent funding source, i.e. the government, the focus tends to shift from fulfilling its stated purpose to maintaining and expanding its budget. When this happens, the institution loses touch with the real world; feedback gets suppressed, hidden or simply ignored as irrelevant.

But feedback from the real world is essential to survival; if we lose feeling in our fingers, we cannot feel the fire and pull away. On the institutional level, another feedback loop arises: if inquiry or market forces threaten the status quo within the institution, the feedback from the real world is attacked as a problem rather than as critically vital information.

In private enterprise, the consequences of any suppression or rejection of feedback from the real world of customers and the market are brutal: the customers abandon the firm and it goes bankrupt. This is the dynamic of Nature, and various companies that rise quickly to fame and fortune and then wither just as quickly illustrate the essential role of feedback.

Presenting a facade of efficiency and fulfillment of purpose does not stave off reality; it only increases the force of the eventual collision between the institution and reality. In China's catastrophically misguided Great Leap Forward in the late 1950s, managers planted rice thickly along certain roadways, and then drove Chairman Mao down these roads to give him the impression that the harvest would be abundant. In fact, the harvest was dismal due to central-government mismanagement, and tens of millions of people starved to death as a direct result of centralized planning and institutional failure.

This highlights the dynamics that constantly work against feedback that threatens the status quo: (1) the human preference for short-term gain even if it leads to long-term disaster, (2) the desire to please those in charge (and thus protect one's own position), and (3) risk cannot be eliminated, it can only be transferred to others.

Institutions transfer the risks of their failure to society and the economy at large. When these organizations make up a small part of the economy, the costs and risks can be distributed thinly enough across the system that the system's stability is not threatened. But when these institutions dominate the economy, the risks being transferred to the system are no longer inconsequential. As Voltaire observed, "No snowflake in an avalanche ever feels responsible." No one in large, centralized institutions, agencies and organizations feels responsible for the systemic risk piling up in the economy.

The successful manager in the emerging economy understands institutional sclerosis and the incentives for opacity and self-service that leads to institutional failure. This manager understands that every snowflake is responsible for the eventual avalanche, and that low-intensity volatility, risk and insecurity is the price of remaining vital and adaptable.

The Community Economy

The obvious advantages of an open market have led many to believe that the competitive marketplace is the solution to all problems. While an open market offers efficiency in many situations, it is not a solution in all situations. The reason is that market-based enterprises exist to reap a profit, and many situations offer no profit potential.

In advanced economies, the market aims to reap profits by commodifying aspects of life that were once provided by the family or community.

Consider what many see as the ideal American lifestyle of a 3,000 square-foot single family home occupied by two adults and a child. Daycare, enrichment and/or private schooling costs $2,000 a month; assisted-living care of an elderly parent costs $5,000 a month; the mortgage on the expansive home costs $3,000 a month; property taxes are $1,000 a month; the two vehicles the family needs to commute to work cost $1,500 a month for loan payments, fuel and maintenance; eating out every week or consuming packaged meals at home costs $1,000 a month; yard and maid service and other domestic services cost $500 a month, and so on. The high income required to pay for all these costs is also heavily taxed, so at least $3,000 a month is paid just in income and sales taxes.

The problem with this lifestyle is that only 5% of the populace can afford it. A solution that only works for the top 5% of the populace is not a solution for the economy or society as a whole.

The market provides the credit, goods and services for every aspect of this idealized life; the community provides nothing and in fact does not exist in this market-based lifestyle.

The state's current solution to this high-cost commodification and marketing of what was once family or community-provided is to borrow roughly a third of every dollar it spends. As we have seen, the demographic tidal wave of retiring Baby Boomers and the decline of paid work will dramatically lower tax revenues while simultaneously increasing expenditures. This double-whammy will upend the state's borrow-and-spend solution.

Digital technologies and social innovation open the possibility of an emergent community economy that depends on neither the for-profit market nor state funding. Such an economy can coexist with a market economy and even a state-cartel system. In effect, it operates on a different system of assessing and measuring value.

The Market and Community Economies

Both the current market economy and the state have replaced the non-market community economy with high-cost solutions that require ever-increasing amounts of credit, income and tax revenues. As the state-cartel economy frays, those solutions will no longer be available to every household.

One way to distinguish between the market economy and the community economy is to consider the stay-at-home parent and the working parent. Both the state and the market benefit when Mom and Dad go to work and pay for the household services they are no longer able to perform: childcare, meal preparation, home and vehicle maintenance, tutoring, and so on. The market wants to provide these services for a profit, and the state wants to collect payroll, income and sales taxes on the money being generated by the working parents and every transaction. But is the family better off paying for services that were once outside the market economy? As paid work becomes scarcer, this question will lose its meaning, for the typical household income will not be enough to fund market-supplied services for all of life.

In traditional societies that we in America tend to dismiss as "Third World", cash income is scarce and so the vast majority of the goods and services of life are generated at home and/or by the community. In such localized economies, where cash is scarce, your home is built with neighbors' help out of local materials, and you reciprocate when your neighbor needs a new roof or house, for example. Food is grown and exchanged for other foodstuffs; surpluses are sold for cash or used in barter. Childcare assistance is provided by older relatives or neighboring parents, again in a reciprocal arrangement. Schooling is often supposed to be paid by the government, but in the real world parents pay fees to the teacher and for supplies. Healthcare is minimal, with herbal treatments and cheap generic medications providing much of the care.

The community marketplace is self-organizing, and social life revolves around the local church or temple, extended families and small-scale family enterprises. Cheap mobile phones and Internet connections provide an extended communications network that ties into distant family and friends, news and the wider world.

Cash is saved for the few food items not grown locally, clothing, mobile phone service, generic medicines, and occasional travel via bus or train.

Many of these features were also standard practice in 19th century and early 20th century America.

It's important to recall here that the secret of a long, prosperous life is well-established: a vibrant social life of friends, family and voluntary associations, a purposeful life (positive reasons to get out of bed in the morning), a diet of whole grains, legumes, fresh fruits and vegetables (lightly processed foods low on the food chain), occasional meat and seafood, and sufficient sleep. None of these requirements require a fortune in cash, and indeed, cash is remarkably irrelevant to social capital such as friendship. (If friendship is based on cash, it isn't friendship.)

Though the pharmaceutical industry has attempted to cure Western lifestyle diseases with high-profit margin medications, it is abundantly evident that a healthy lifestyle cannot be replaced by a handful of pills. A billion dollars of biochemical research and development will not be able to duplicate the health benefits and well-being of a purposeful life, a caring community and a healthy lifestyle and diet.

From the long view of human society, we are in a peculiarly alienated era, one where the foundation of community has been lost to the encroachment of the state and market. The Internet has enabled an interconnected, globally empowered community: local services can be distributed across the globe digitally, ideas can be traded across borders, and new technologies and skills made available for the cost of an Internet connection and a relatively modest quantity of electricity.

The idea that a relocalized community-based economy is the foundation of well-being and prosperity runs counter to the two dominant forces in our economy and society, the central state and the globalized market. As a result, the possibility that an Internet-connected community could deliver goods and services for a fraction of the cost of the status quo is still very much on the margins. That may change as the current system stagnates.

The Pareto Economy

In what I call the Pareto Economy, the focus is on the vital 20% investment of financial and human capital that can yield 80% of the potential benefit. In this model, the cost of living can be slashed by up to 80% while retaining the essentials of a rewarding, healthy life by investing in what we might call "good enough."

In stark contrast, the state-cartel model pursues diminishing return, frequently spending vast sums in an attempt to capture the last few percentage points of potential profit.

As noted previously, many significant reductions in cost and inefficiency can be reaped from behavioral changes that require little capital investment or new technology. The built environment of homes, commercial areas, roadways, etc., offers many opportunities for such dramatic reductions in cost and resources.

In the current debt-based consumerist model, a three-person household might occupy a 3,000 square foot dwelling. In the emerging economy/community model, three households might share that space, instantly reducing housing costs by two-thirds. It might be several generations in one home or some variation of that (parent, offspring and a couple of their friends) or three voluntary housemates.

Sharing buildings is intrinsically more efficient and cost-effective than large homes occupied by one or two people. Sharing space also means that maintenance expenses are shared, and some sort of social life and reciprocity is built-in.

In the current consumerist model, each household typically owns a costly vehicle for each adult. In the shared social unit, five families might share one vehicle, a city block might share a pickup truck for occasional use, or everyone has access to a vehicle from one of the many car-sharing companies. This access not ownership model will reduce vehicle costs by up to 80% per household.

Other transport options include walking, bicycling and a wide range of lightweight, low-cost wheeled vehicles from urban golf-carts to electric mopeds to enclosed tricycles.

If the shared dwelling has a mortgage, it could be crowd-funded: individual investors could review the household's finances and the attributes of the property, and invest directly in a pooled mortgage. The interest and principal would be automatically calculated and distributed with open-source software. No bank would collect fees or interest, and the mortgage would not be financialized (i.e. divided into tranches and sold as mortgage-backed securities).

The community labor bank described earlier offers an effective model for the Community economy. Those with little cash income offer their labor to the exchange to bank hours of service which they can then trade for other's labor or for goods that have been offered in exchange for labor. Those needing labor for any legal, non-exploitive purpose will be able to request unpaid labor from the bank. For example, if one of the new owners of a derelict building banked 100 hours in unpaid labor helping others with yard work and tutoring, he could then request 100 hours of equivalently skilled labor from others in the labor bank.

This model of community exchange can be expanded to include goods. For example, a community member might have a surplus of vegetables from her garden which she would offer online in the exchange, where someone wanting the produce might offer hours of labor in trade. The owner would get the labor she needs, not necessarily from the person who traded labor for her garden produce, but from another member in the exchange.

The community labor/goods exchange is a highly flexible, scalable model that lends itself to automated software and transparency. It enables full community-based employment in a largely cash-free, non-market economy that would flourish in parallel with the market economy.

If someone has cash and wants to hire a person for a wage, they will be free to do so. If cash is scarce, the community labor/goods exchange would enable every member to trade for other's expertise and locally produced goods and services.

Though severely disabled people would be unable to contribute, the majority of people currently classified as disabled by states agencies could still contribute in a meaningful fashion. For example, a partially disabled member might be able to contribute computer skills to the community or provide "eyes on the street" security along with other less mobile members of the community.

Though process costs and labor costs per unit of manufacture are declining globally as robotics and software replace human labor, the localized maker economy could offer opportunities to earn money in the marketplace. The cost of digital fabrication equipment is dropping rapidly, and the access-not-ownership model provides a template for pooling community resources to buy equipment that can be rented/shared by makers for a modest fee.

We can also anticipate new opportunities for community/municipality coordination. Street repair might be one such service. The city might supply the materials, equipment and one crew supervisor, while the rest of the labor could be provided by volunteers who bank their unpaid hours at the community labor/goods exchange.

Local permaculture-based production of produce and food services offer a decentralized, diversified range of opportunities to generate income. Though small-scale agriculture in America is still generally dismissed as "too small to make financial sense," in other countries small home plots, rooftop gardens, etc. supply half or more of the nation's seasonal produce.

This illustrates the need to differentiate between value and price. The value of local food security cannot be captured by price until that security has been lost to crazy low prices of imported food. At that point, high prices only reflect the incomplete information provided by the previously crazy low prices.

The Community economy recognizes that not every task worth doing has a market value, though it may provide a significant non-marketable value to the community.

Hybrid Work

What I term hybrid work is a dynamic mix of paid, unpaid, self-directed and collaborative projects that yield a steady stream of cash or banked labor that can be traded for labor or goods. Hybrid work is the natural result of interconnected market and community economies.

In the hybrid work model (also called patchwork careers), each person chooses their own mix of productive work. Some projects may generate cash income; others may generate bankable value via the labor bank. Hybrid work recognizes that not all value creation occurs in a marketplace, and that reciprocity and purpose provide meaning, self-worth and opportunities for self-cultivation and building human/social capital.

Hybrid work offers intrinsic resilience and security by distributing risk and creating value across a spectrum of projects and networks.

In one sense, the Nearly Free University project of preparing students to establish and maintain a livelihood in the emerging economy can be understood as preparing students to thrive in the community/market economy of hybrid work where value creation takes many forms.

Matching Work and Workers: Adaptive Employment

Just as the Nearly Free University model individualizes learning by aligning the personality, aptitudes, interests and preferences of each student and uses open-source automated software to deliver this model at low cost, the Emerging Economy seeks to connect each individual with work that aligns with their personality, aptitudes, training, experience and interests. This currently haphazard process of matching workers and work could be largely automated if sufficient resources were invested in such a network of adaptive employment.

The hybrid/patchwork model enables a much finer-grained alignment of work and worker; rather than try to find an increasingly scarce conventional full-time job for every worker, the Emerging Economy model of matching work and worker enables flexible scheduling and the potential individuals to perform a variety of work in a variety of settings.

Just as the factory model of education has become obsolete, so too has the factory model of each individual performing the same task in the same institution for their entire career become obsolete in much of the Emerging Economy. Technology is enabling a much more accurate assessment of each individual's aptitudes, personality, experience and interests, and a broader, more flexible project-based approach to work. Aligning individuals to work that suits them has the potential to greatly increase productivity, wealth and happiness.

Conclusion

We now understand the integral unity of the emerging economy and The Nearly Free University. While many will question the need for such a radical reset of higher education and the economy, questions of need miss the entire point of Chapters 3, 4 and 5, which is that the current economy is unsustainable and a reset to a more sustainable model will occur regardless of our unwillingness to accept this inevitability.

Our choices for addressing this reality narrow down to (1) attempting to sustain what is unsustainable; (2) squandering remaining resources on a futile diminishing-return quest, or (3) embracing the emerging economy and the social innovations it is spawning.

It would be impossible in the space of one book to discuss every possible facet of all the current issues in our existing higher education system and economy. Instead, I have tried to touch on the most salient issues and sketch the outlines of emerging solutions worthy of further debate and consideration. If we are indeed entering a period of systemic instability and tumultuous transformation, we cannot possibly predict the eventual outcome, other than to note the unlikelihood that everything remains exactly as it is this September day in 2013.

Eras of systemic transformation place a high premium on adaptability above all other traits, verifying Darwin's observation that "It is not the strongest of the species that survives, or the most intelligent, but the ones most adaptable to change."

The Nearly Free University is a manifestation of the emerging economy that places precisely this premium on adaptability, resourcefulness and all the attributes of resilient systems: efficient use of resources, low fixed costs, a messy, fast-evolving structure that is flexible and adaptable, a low cost of innovation, a high bandwidth for collaboration, a systemic tolerance for risk-taking and low-level volatility, and a rapid uptake of the lessons learned from analysis and failure.

The Nearly Free University's evolutionary pathway is unknown; what is known is that we desperately need to encourage and enable the evolution of both the Nearly Free University and the emerging economy it serves, lest the old order's dissolution leaves us bereft of everything required in the new order.

Charles Hugh Smith

Berkeley, California

September, 2013

Made in the USA
Lexington, KY
23 July 2014